Making History

Making HISTORY

Interviews with four generals of
Cuba's Revolutionary Armed Forces

Preface by Juan Almeida Bosque

Introduction by Mary-Alice Waters

Pathfinder
New York London Montreal Sydney

Edited by Mary-Alice Waters

Copyright © 1999 by Pathfinder Press

ISBN 0-87348-902-0 paper; ISBN 0-87348-903-9 cloth
Library of Congress Catalog Card Number 99-95110

Manufactured in the United States of America

First edition, 1999
Second printing, revised, 2000

COVER PHOTO: Militia members in Havana during January 1961
   mobilization of some 40,000 volunteers to counter heightened danger of
   U.S. attack during transition from President Dwight D. Eisenhower to
   John F. Kennedy. (Raúl Corrales)
COVER DESIGN: Eva Braiman

Pathfinder
410 West Street, New York, NY 10014, U.S.A.
Fax: (212) 727-0150
E-mail: pathfinderpress@compuserve.com

PATHFINDER DISTRIBUTORS AROUND THE WORLD:
Australia (and Asia and the Pacific):
   Pathfinder, 1st floor, 176 Redfern St., Redfern, NSW 2016
   Postal address: P.O. Box K879, Haymarket, NSW 1240
Canada:
   Pathfinder, 851 Bloor St. West, Toronto, ON, M6G 1M3
Iceland:
   Pathfinder, Klapparstíg 26, 2d floor, 101 Reykjavík
   Postal address: P. Box 0233, IS 121 Reykjavík
New Zealand:
   Pathfinder, La Gonda Arcade, 203 Karangahape Road, Auckland
   Postal address: P.O. Box 8730, Auckland
Sweden:
   Pathfinder, Vikingagatan 10, S-113 42, Stockholm
United Kingdom (and Europe, Africa except South Africa, and Middle East):
   Pathfinder, 47 The Cut, London, SE1 8LL
United States (and Caribbean, Latin America, and South Africa):
   Pathfinder, 410 West Street, New York, NY 10014

Contents

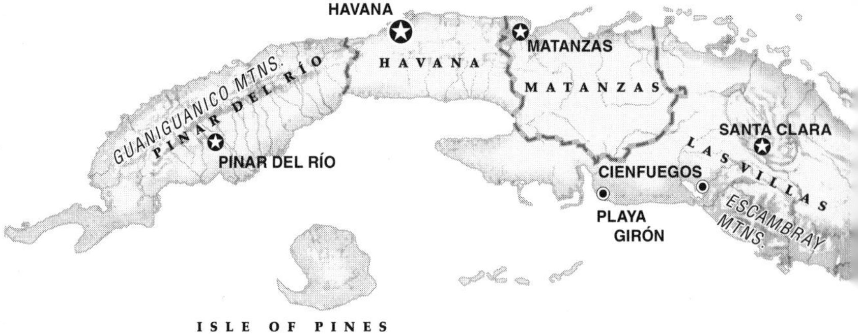
HAVANA
HAVANA
MATANZAS
MATANZAS
GUANIGUANICO MTNS.
PINAR DEL RÍO
PINAR DEL RÍO
SANTA CLARA
LAS VILLAS
CIENFUEGOS
PLAYA GIRÓN
ESCAMBRAY MTNS.
ISLE OF PINES

Cuba 1959

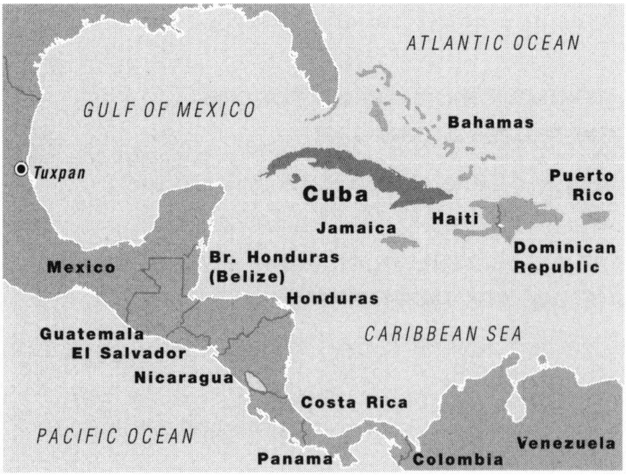
ATLANTIC OCEAN
GULF OF MEXICO
Bahamas
Tuxpan
Cuba
Puerto Rico
Haiti
Jamaica
Dominican Republic
Mexico
Br. Honduras (Belize)
Honduras
Guatemala
El Salvador
CARIBBEAN SEA
Nicaragua
Costa Rica
PACIFIC OCEAN
Panama
Colombia
Venezuela

CAMAGÜEY

CAMAGÜEY

O R I E N T E

SAGUA-BARACOA MTNS.

SIERRA MAESTRA

SANTIAGO DE CUBA

GUANTÁNAMO NAVAL BASE

160 KILOMETERS

100 MILES

Preface

THE INTERVIEWS WITH FOUR GENERALS of the Revolutionary Armed Forces of Cuba contained in *Making History* present us, in simple language, the impressions of these combatants on the topics selected, based on their own experiences.

The four are examples of ordinary individuals from among the Cuban people, different only in their responsibilities and military specialization, as well as their origin and the historic role each has played during these forty years of revolution.

Through their answers and accounts, they identify important moments in our history, describe their reasons for joining the revolution, and tell of aspects of our people's struggle. One can perceive the simple honesty of these men, who deeply love the cause they fight for, who are loyal and fair toward Raúl in responding to questions about his work as minister of the FAR, and who stand firmly with Fidel as guide, educator, and central leader of our revolution.

I salute the effort of the interviewers and anticipate that readers will be grateful for, and moved by, the living recollections of these four generals.

Juan Almeida Bosque
Commander of the Revolution

December 1999

Introduction

*"We have been capable of making history
but not of writing it."*

Raúl Castro

ON JANUARY 1, 1959, men and women of Cuba in their millions ceased being simply the objects of history and became its makers as well. In so doing they opened the door to the first socialist revolution in the Americas.

As the four interviews in this book highlight, the human beings who fought to accomplish that feat were ordinary working people. Overwhelmingly young, most still in their teens or early twenties—workers, farmers, students, shopkeepers—they didn't set out to change world history. They had merely decided to bring down by any means necessary the bloody tyranny of Fulgencio Batista—a dictatorship backed by the military might of Washington and the propertied interests it represents.

As the revolutionary war unfolded from late 1956 on, victory was decided by the caliber of the Rebel Army soldiers forged under the command of Fidel Castro. Where the men and women who emerged as the leading cadre of the Rebel Army came from, and what shaped them, is the real subject of this book. As generals of Cuba's Revolutionary Armed Forces (FAR) talk about their experiences, we get a glimpse of how the struggle itself transformed them, changing their understanding of the world and their place in it and creating the disciplined communist fighters whose unity has both led the

Cuban people forward and held U.S. imperialism at bay for more than four decades.

"The Cuban revolution you see today continues, but is not the same as, the Cuban revolution of yesterday, even after the victory," the Argentine-born Cuban leader Ernesto Che Guevara told a thousand young people from throughout the Americas gathered in Havana the summer of 1960 for the historic first Latin American Youth Congress.

> Much less is it the Cuban insurrection prior to the victory, at the time when those eighty-two youth made the difficult crossing of the Gulf of Mexico in a boat taking on water, to reach the shores of the Sierra Maestra. Between those youth and the representatives of Cuba today there is a distance that cannot be measured in years—or at least not correctly measured in years, with twenty-four-hour days and sixty-minute hours.
>
> All the members of the Cuban government—young in age, young in character, and young in the illusions they had—have nevertheless matured in the extraordinary school of experience, in living contact with the people, with their needs and aspirations.
>
> The hope all of us had was to arrive one day somewhere in Cuba, and after a few shouts, a few heroic actions, a few deaths, and a few radio broadcasts, to take power and drive out the dictator Batista. History showed us it was much more difficult to overthrow a whole government backed by an army of murderers—murderers who were partners of that government and were backed by the greatest colonial power on earth.
>
> That was how, little by little, all our ideas changed.

■

In April 1997 a team of reporters for the *Militant* newspaper and the Spanish-language magazine *Perspectiva Mundial,* both published in New York, visited Cuba. Reminiscences and analyses of the victory of the Cuban militias and Revolutionary Armed Forces at Playa Girón on the Bay of Pigs were in the news, as the thirty-sixth anniversary of that titanic accomplishment approached.

On April 17, 1961, an expeditionary force of some 1,500 Cuban mercenaries, armed, organized, and financed by the U.S. government, landed in an isolated area of south-central Cuba with the objective of establishing a beachhead, declaring a provisional government, and appealing to Washington for immediate military support. Within seventy-two hours the invading troops were routed and virtually the entire force taken captive. The beachhead was never consolidated. Cuban commander in chief Fidel Castro rightly referred to this battle as the first military defeat of Yankee imperialism in Latin America.

Our reporting team mentioned to colleagues in Cuba that we would like to write something for our readers commemorating that historic event. When asked if we would be interested in interviewing some veterans of the combat at Playa Girón, we said yes, enthusiastically. Within a matter of days, much to our surprise, the combatants with whom interviews had been arranged turned out to be three division and brigadier generals of the Revolutionary Armed Forces of Cuba— José Ramón Fernández, field commander of the Cuban forces at Playa Girón; Enrique Carreras, who commanded Cuba's air force in that battle; and Néstor López Cuba, one of the tank corps commanders.

The interviews actually occurred a few months later, in October 1997. By chance they coincided with the anniversary of the 1962 October Crisis, known in the United States as the "Missile" Crisis. Thirty-five years earlier, the administration of John F. Kennedy had pushed the world to the brink of nuclear war in a showdown with the governments of Cuba and the Soviet Union over the installation of Soviet nuclear weapons—accepted by Cuba in face of the need to defend the island from Washington's mounting invasion preparations. This anniversary, too, was much in the news, both in the

United States and Cuba, and was an unexpected opportunity to ask the three generals not only about combat at the Bay of Pigs, but about their experiences at the time of the October Crisis as well.

October 1997 was an important moment in Cuba's history. Solemn ceremonies from Havana to Santa Clara and beyond commemorated the return to Cuba of the remains of Ernesto Che Guevara and six other internationalist combatants who had fought alongside him in Bolivia in 1966–67 in the effort he led to consolidate a revolutionary leadership nucleus in the Southern Cone of Latin America. In his speech to the main ceremony in Santa Clara where the remains of these internationalist fighters were laid to rest, President Fidel Castro said he viewed "Che and his men as reinforcements, as a detachment of invincible combatants that this time includes not just Cubans. It also includes Latin Americans who have come to fight at our side and to write new pages of history and glory."

In addition to the three commanders at Playa Girón, we were able to interview one of the combatants in the Bolivian campaign: Brigadier General Harry Villegas. "Pombo," as he is known worldwide, served on Guevara's general staff in Bolivia, and following Guevara's death commanded the Cuban and Bolivian revolutionaries who fought their way out of the military encirclement organized by the Bolivian army and U.S. special forces.

Generals of the FAR have given few interviews over the years to Cuban, let alone non-Cuban reporters. The four generals placed no restrictions on the topics or questions to be posed to them, however, nor did they ask for questions in advance. The interviews at times took on the character of a conversation and exchange. Revolutionaries from the United States and Cuba talked about history-making events, some of which they had lived through in common from very different vantage points in the frontline trenches.

From their earliest political experiences in the struggle against the Batista dictatorship; to their participation in the epic combat of David against the Goliath of U.S. imperialism throughout the opening years of the revolution; to their internationalist missions in parts of the world as far removed from each other as Syria, Vietnam, Bolivia, the Congo, Nicaragua, and Angola; to their observations about the challenges facing the Cuban revolution today—the generals spoke with candor and clarity.

Four things above all stand out.

First, as Fidel Castro has often remarked, Cuba's Revolutionary Armed Forces didn't learn the art of war by reading manuals in the classrooms of a military academy. "They are forces whose roots are in history and whose apprenticeship was in combat," he noted on April 19, 1963, the second anniversary of the defeat of U.S. imperialism at the Bay of Pigs. Cuban men and women fought for something they believed in—and combined that experience, as soon as time permitted, with the study and training that have made the FAR among the most feared and most admired armies in the world, depending on one's class standpoint.

"This revolution has been characterized not by being a copier but by being a creator," Fidel told the July 26 rally in Santiago de Cuba in 1988. "Had we been willing to follow the schemas, we would not be gathered here today, we would not have had July 26, we would not have had a socialist revolution in this hemisphere. . . . Theory had it that no revolution could be made here. . . . That's what the manuals used to say."

Second, the fact that the majority of the cadres of the Revolutionary Armed Forces, including its officers, came from peasant and working-class origins is a product of the actual development of the Rebel Army over the course of the 1956–58 revolutionary war. The deliberate measures by Cuba's leadership to maintain that social composition are an expression of the class interests the FAR defends.

The heartfelt revulsion expressed in these interviews over the contemptuous and dehumanizing treatment of soldiers by officers in other armies, as witnessed by some of the generals, underscores the class character and composition of the FAR. This character is registered above all in the internationalism of the Cuban revolution. "Whoever is incapable of fighting for others will never be capable of fighting for himself," was the way Fidel Castro summarized this touchstone of the revolution in a speech to half a million people in Havana on Cuba's Armed Forces Day in December 1988.

Third, these interviews highlight the decisive place of youth in the forging of the revolutionary movement in Cuba. Two of the generals were themselves teenagers when they joined the Rebel Army in the Sierra Maestra. The preponderance of young fighters carrying the full range of military and political responsibilities in the revolutionary government following the triumph in 1959 is evident.

Fourth, the heroic days of the Cuban revolution are not past, but are present and future. The extremely difficult economic conditions since the early 1990s referred to in Cuba as the Special Period pose challenges as great as any the revolution has ever faced, especially political challenges. That is why the accurate history of the Cuban revolution and its Revolutionary Armed Forces, as told by living combatants, becomes even more important to the continuity needed so much by young revolutionary fighters.

As the generals interviewed here explain and exemplify, the seeds of the revolutionary discipline, selfless attitudes, and commitment to human solidarity that mark the vanguard in Cuba today were planted in the earliest years of the struggle against the Batista dictatorship. Many institutions, including the FAR itself, the militias, and the Union of Young Communists trace their origins in a straight line to the Rebel Army—which also gave birth to policies as wide-ranging as the revolution's priority to advancing the literacy and culture of the toilers, its measures to combat racial discrimination and promote women's equality, and its profound agrarian revolution.

In the initial years following the triumph in 1959, the cadres of Cuba's revolutionary movement did not have the leisure, nor did many of the workers and peasants who were making history yet have the cultural level, that would have enabled them to also write it down for others. That task is now consciously and deliberately being shouldered by the revolutionary leadership. The fruits of this endeavor are important not just for the people of Cuba, but for workers, farmers, and youth throughout the Americas and around the world who seek to emulate the example of the Cuban revolution. *Making History*, we hope, is a modest contribution to this effort.

■

A special note of appreciation is due to Santiago Dórquez, director of Editora Política, as well as Iraida Aguirrechu, Nora Madan, and others there whose aid and collaboration made possible not only the interviews in this volume but their careful editing as well.

Readers for whom the many historical references in these pages are largely new or unfamiliar will find the extensive combined glossary and notes at the end of the volume especially useful. Similarly, the notes on further reading will be an aid for those who wish to delve more deeply into the lessons of the modern working-class movement that form the historical framework assumed by the four Cuban generals and referred to in their remarks.

We dedicate this volume to the young people of Cuba and worldwide, for whom the men and women of the Rebel Army still point the way.

Mary-Alice Waters
October 1999

About the interviewers

Jack Barnes, national secretary of the Socialist Workers Party, is author of *Capitalism's World Disorder: Working-Class Politics at the Millennium; The Changing Face of U.S. Politics;* "U.S. Imperialism Has Lost the Cold War"; *For a Workers and Farmers Government in the United States;* and "The Politics of Economics: Che Guevara and Marxist Continuity."

Mary-Alice Waters, president of Pathfinder Press, is editor of the Marxist magazine *New International.* She is author of "Defending Cuba, Defending Cuba's Socialist Revolution," and is editor of *Rosa Luxemburg Speaks; Cosmetics, Fashions, and the Exploitation of Women;* as well as numerous books of speeches and writings by Fidel Castro and Ernesto Che Guevara.

Martín Koppel is editor of the Spanish-language monthly magazine *Perspectiva Mundial* and of *Nueva Internacional.* He is also the editor of *Puerto Rico: Independence Is a Necessity* by Rafael Cancel Miranda.

'The Cuban people remain armed and ready to defend the revolution'

DIVISION GENERAL NÉSTOR LÓPEZ CUBA

MARTÍN KOPPEL/MILITANT

COURTESY NÉSTOR LÓPEZ CUBA

Top: Div. Gen. Néstor López Cuba during interview.

Bottom: López Cuba (third person from left, facing camera and wearing hat) in Angola, 1976, at the Namibian border. Men with backs to camera are South Africans. At right, Cuban officer Jorge Guerrero.

Néstor López Cuba

Div. gen. néstor lópez cuba was born in 1938 into a peasant family near the city of Holguín, in what was then the province of Oriente in eastern Cuba. He attended school up to the sixth grade when his father told him, "School is in town, and peasants get corrupted in town. Pick up your machete and hoe and help me here in the fields." For the next several years the young man did so, working also as a sugarcane cutter, cart driver, and truck loader.

In 1957 López Cuba joined a cell of the July 26 Revolutionary Movement, which was leading the struggle in Cuba to bring down the U.S.-backed dictatorship of Fulgencio Batista. One of the cell's most important activities was raising money for the Rebel Army, led by Fidel Castro, which from its base in the Sierra Maestra mountains of eastern Cuba, had begun waging a revolutionary war against the Batista tyranny.

In May 1958, as repression by the regime intensified, López Cuba and a group of his comrades went up to the mountains to join the Rebel Army. They became members of a front led by Raúl Castro, taking part in the Rebel Army counteroffensive in late 1958 that culminated in a triumphant popular uprising and general strike. In face of these developments, Batista fled Cuba on January 1, 1959.

When he heard the news of Batista's flight, López Cuba assumed the job was done. His unit was stationed only twenty-five miles from his father's farm. When his brothers came looking for him, he turned in his military gear, and prepared to go home. "I'm off," he told his fellow combatants. "The war is over and I'm going back to the fields."

His commander, Abelardo Colomé Ibarra—known, then as now, as "Furry"—learned of this and spoke with López Cuba.

"No, you can't go," Colomé told him. "Are you chicken? How can you take off when things are just beginning?"

"Come with us," the commander insisted. "You can return when the situation permits."

He wasn't chicken. López Cuba joined the Liberty Caravan that marched with Rebel Army commander in chief Fidel Castro from Oriente province to Havana, Cuba's capital. They arrived January 8.

López Cuba never returned to the life of a farmer.

He soon became head of the Rebel Army's first tank battalion. In October 1960 the first Soviet tanks requested by the Cuban government to defend the revolution against escalating U.S. attacks began to arrive. The Rebel Army immediately organized a crash course in how to operate them. "Everything we learned in the morning from the Soviet instructors we had to teach at night to the rest of the compañeros," he later recalled. Before they had finished their training course, U.S.-organized counterrevolutionaries launched the Bay of Pigs invasion.

On the morning of April 17, 1961, López Cuba, not yet knowing of the mercenary attack, was ordered to move immediately to Matanzas at the head of a tank contingent. When he reached this destination, he was startled to find himself face to face with Commander in Chief Fidel Castro, who told him of the invasion at Playa Girón and ordered the unit into battle.

With four functioning tanks, the squad advanced, accompanied by militia units on foot. They saw heavy combat and helped contain the initial advance of the invading mercenaries, who were defeated within seventy-two hours by the Revolutionary Armed Forces and popular militias.

López Cuba himself was wounded by enemy machine gun fire. His comrades took him to a field hospital, from which they planned to evacuate him to Matanzas for an operation to remove shrapnel lodged in his arm.

As he listened to other wounded fighters tell of the advance of the revolutionary troops at Playa Girón, however, López Cuba got out of his hospital bed and headed back to the battlefield. He was present for the final push against the invading forces, until Castro, noticing that López Cuba was suffering chills and fever, ordered him off the field. After the battle he was promoted to the rank of captain.

In 1973 López Cuba volunteered for a mission in Syria, at the head of a tank battalion that later became a regiment. That year Syrian and Egyptian forces had fought a war against the Israeli army to try to retake the Golan Heights and Israeli-occupied territory in the Sinai desert. While the Cuban internationalist military mission did not see combat, it organized fortification of Syrian defenses, helping deter further Israeli aggression. The unit remained in Syria until February 1975.

Shortly after returning to Cuba, López Cuba joined the first Cuban internationalist volunteers who arrived in Angola in late 1975, responding to the urgent request of the government of that newly independent country for help in combating a South African invasion. His tank column opened the way across Angola as the advance detachment of the Cuban forces, reaching the border with Namibia—then a South African colony—in March 1976. The apartheid regime was forced to shelve its plans for a quick military defeat of Angola.

A thirteen-year effort to wear down the Angolan government and Cuban internationalists ensued, with the South African military spearheading support for a bloody war waged by right-wing Angolan forces. More than 300,000 Cuban volunteers fought in Angola over this period; 2,000 were killed.

In 1988, at the battle of Cuito Cuanavale, another direct South African invasion was defeated by Cuban volunteers, Angolan troops, and Namibian fighters. A weakened South African regime sued for peace in Angola and conceded independence to

Namibia in 1990. By 1994 apartheid itself had succumbed to a sustained rise in mass struggles inspired in part by the victory over South African forces at Cuito Cuanavale.

Following the July 1979 victory of the Nicaraguan revolution, López Cuba headed the Cuban military mission in Nicaragua. In response to the request of the new government, the Cuban mission assisted and advised the Sandinista army in defending the revolution and the sovereignty of Nicaragua against the U.S.-backed mercenary forces known as the "contras."

The interview with López Cuba was conducted in Havana, Cuba, on October 20, 1997, by Jack Barnes, Mary-Alice Waters, and Martín Koppel.

At the time, López Cuba was head of the Political Directorate of the Revolutionary Armed Forces of Cuba, a member of the Central Committee of the Communist Party of Cuba, and a deputy of the National Assembly of People's Power. In December 1998 he was elected vice president of the Executive Secretariat of the Association of Combatants of the Cuban Revolution. He held these responsibilities at the time of his death on October 15, 1999.

'The Cuban people remain armed and ready to defend the revolution'

MARY-ALICE WATERS: We would like to begin by asking you about the interviews with some forty generals of the Revolutionary Armed Forces published earlier this year in the book *Secretos de generales*. How did these come about?

NÉSTOR LÓPEZ CUBA: Since the first years after the revolution's triumph, our leaders, the commander in chief [Fidel Castro] and the minister [of the armed forces, Raúl Castro], have said that we were capable of making history but not of writing it.

Writing was quite difficult for those of us in the Rebel Army, since almost all of us were peasants and workers, with a low cultural level. Even if we had wanted to devote ourselves to writing history during the first years of the revolution, I believe it would have been impossible, given our lack of skills.

What's more, since the very first days of the revolution we faced constant threats. We had to remain by our tanks, by our artillery, training and preparing ourselves. Because we knew an attack was imminent. That's another very powerful reason.

During those early years, Che wrote a little about the *guerrilla*, about the experience of the guerrillas. He wrote *Socialism and Man in Cuba*. Some diaries, such as those by Almeida and Che and Raúl, had been filed away somewhere and not released publicly; they began to be published sometime after the twentieth anniversary of the revolution, and around the thirtieth anniversary of the *Granma* landing.[1]

The first years were difficult. We had no arms. We tried to get them from capitalist countries, but they sabotaged our efforts to do so. Later, at the end of 1960, arms began to arrive from the Soviet Union and the socialist camp. We continued the difficult task of training ourselves, of preparing ourselves, because everything pointed to an imminent attack.

In April 1961 the first invasion took place at Playa Girón. Of course, there had been acts of sabotage even before that, in 1959 and 1960. Our sugar mills and plantations had been bombed. The freighter *La Coubre* was blown up, together with its shipment of arms we had purchased from Belgium at enormous effort. The funds for antiaircraft weapons had been collected from the people.

The struggle made it impossible for the protagonists of that early chapter of the Rebel Army to write things down.

Later our country began to strengthen itself defensively. The relations we had with the socialist camp were a big help in improving our economy a bit. We were training ourselves, studying, raising our skill level. We now faced a different situation.

Our internationalist missions began, and they were very complex during the first years. Beginning in 1963 we aided Algeria, and then came our support to some of the liberation movements in Africa. The missions became a little more massive in Syria in 1973, in Angola in 1975, in Ethiopia in 1977.[2]

---

1 Names and events referred to in these interviews are identified in the notes at the back of the book.

2 In 1963 Cuban troops went to Algeria, at the request of the revolutionary government of Ahmed Ben Bella, to combat an imperialist-inspired invasion of that country by Morocco. In 1965 Cuban volunteers led by Che Guevara fought alongside forces in the Congo against U.S.-backed Belgian and South African mercenaries—one of numerous such operations to aid African liberation movements over the years. In 1977 Cuba responded to a request by the government of Ethiopia to help defeat a U.S.-backed invasion by the regime in neighboring Somalia aimed at seizing the Ogaden region. Washington planned

Through the international assistance we were providing other nations, we were accumulating many years of military training, of schooling. We were raising our cultural level and, of course, our combat experience. And that's leaving aside our own guerrilla experience of 1957 and 1958.

Our Rebel Army had by now become a more modern armed force—more capable, better trained, with an educated cadre.

Beginning many years ago the journalist Luis Báez started insisting that something had to be written about our armed forces. There were years of attempts, but no results. So that's where the idea came from. Báez raised this with Almeida in 1994 and Almeida consulted Raúl. Raúl liked the idea, because he had always thought we should write down our experiences.

Previously there had been no interviews with generals except about particular historical dates and events. Then the anniversary of Girón came around, and there were interviews about the individual experiences of each of us at Girón. And that's when the book was authorized—to collect together interviews with a group of generals.

Preparing the book was not an easy task, of course. Because when you read it, or if you have already read it, you'll see that the interviews contain things our people themselves didn't know about, and that were completely new for the rest of the world. They contain things that had been kept on a need-to-know basis, held in the strictest secrecy.

The minister [Raúl Castro] was asked whether the interviews could be completely open. Would we be able to tell all? And he said yes, there would be no restrictions. Some interviews are a little longer than others, more extensive, but they were all cut down a little.

The book, of course, does not include all the generals; we have ninety or a hundred generals, and there are interviews

---

to use a Somalian victory as a springboard to help turn back land redistribution and other measures that had been taken in Ethiopia following the overthrow of the landlord-based monarchy of Emperor Haile Selassie in 1974.

with only forty-one of us in the book. In addition, there is a group of combatants who were commanders of the Rebel Army, heads of columns in the Sierra. An effort is now being made to collect together interviews with them, so that none of their experiences are lost. Many of these compañeros are now retired, but they have rich experiences to tell about, since they played a decisive role in the fight against the Batista tyranny.

That is why the interviews have had such an impact on the population. Because there are things in them that I and other compañeros tell about that not even our families, not even our wives or children, knew beforehand. This has been very valuable for the Cuban people, as well as for our friends abroad, who have learned many things for the first time.

October 1962 'missile' crisis

JACK BARNES: As you know, the way the history of the 1962 October Crisis is written in the United States, [U.S. president John] Kennedy and [Soviet premier Nikita] Khrushchev saved the world from nuclear holocaust. But we have always told people that the truth lies elsewhere. It was the Cuban people and its Revolutionary Armed Forces that saved the world.

Kennedy fully intended to mount an invasion of Cuba in October 1962, as he had been planning to do for more than a year. Previously classified documents released in the past few years, however, show that his hand was stayed when the Pentagon informed him that he could expect an estimated 18,000 U.S. troop casualties during the first ten days alone of an invasion. The Cuban people were armed and mobilized on a massive scale, Kennedy was told by the Joint Chiefs of Staff. The Cuban army was large for a small country, and, together with the militias, very combat-ready.

Kennedy feared the domestic political consequences as a flood of body bags began coming home. So that's when he started seriously probing Khrushchev for a deal.

Just two nights ago, Mary-Alice and I spoke at a public meeting in Chicago that was a send-off for this trip to Cuba.

There were over a hundred workers and youth in attendance, and we told them that among other things we would be interviewing several generals of the FAR while we were here. And we promised we would pass along to you our conviction, as revolutionists who work and fight in the United States, that the Cuban people and their armed forces saved the world in 1962, because you were ready to fight.

So we'd like to ask you about where you were during the October Crisis and your memory of the response by workers and farmers, in and out of uniform, during those days.

LÓPEZ CUBA: It's very true, as you say, that the armed forces, and the people of Cuba above all, played a decisive role in preventing a nuclear holocaust. Because it was understood in Washington that the people would fight and the invasion would be costly. This has been the attitude of our people from the triumph of the revolution until today, I believe. Had this consciousness not existed, they would have invaded us.

At the time of Girón, there is no question that [former U.S. president Dwight] Eisenhower had bequeathed the mercenary brigades to Kennedy, and Kennedy had to support them in the invasion. The one decision Kennedy made on his own was not to land the U.S. Marines behind the mercenaries. Had Eisenhower been in power, we believe, things would have been different; they would have sent in the marines. But Kennedy had just become president, and I think this made him stop and think a bit.

The North Americans have presented their version of the October Crisis. The Russians have told theirs. Cuba has issued important statements and published documents, above all during the conference held in Havana on the thirtieth anniversary of the crisis, attended by Fidel and McNamara, but we have not yet said our final word.[3]

3 A conference on the October 1962 "missile crisis" was held in Havana January 9–12, 1992, involving contemporary participants in those events from the Cuban, U.S., and Soviet governments.

I believe that much remains to be told about the events of the October Crisis, about the role played by Fidel, the leadership of the revolution, our people, and the armed forces.

Of course, the fact that many documents have now been declassified in the United States and Russia adds new elements that make our position much clearer.

In any case, leaving aside the decisions taken by both the U.S. and Soviet governments—both of them nuclear powers—I believe the stance and position of the Cuban people and its armed forces in defending Cuba during the crisis played a decisive role. That factor carried a lot of weight in the decisions made by both governments, especially the United States government.

Now, let me turn to your question about what I was doing during the October Crisis. After Girón I went to the Soviet Union to take my first study course for tank crews. That's where I was when the October Crisis hit. So I was not one of the protagonists in those events.

At military academy in Russia

BARNES: Perhaps you can tell us what the atmosphere was like among the Cubans who were in Russia during the crisis? And among those in the Russian military who were training you?

LÓPEZ CUBA: Well, information began to arrive immediately. Those of us at the military academy were told that the instructions from Cuba were for us to remain calm, that there were sufficient forces there to solve the problem.

But we planned to hijack a plane from the Moscow airport and return to Cuba. This coincided with a visit by Che to Africa, so our leaders sent him to Moscow to meet with us and calm us down, since they knew we were prepared to return to Cuba at all costs. We were ready to head to the airport and seize a plane by force, militarily. We were going to steal the guns from the stockade at the school. But we had it all planned, because we knew we were not going to be allowed to leave otherwise.

That was the situation. But there was something else. We had already spent eight months at the academy, and were well liked by the teachers and personnel, who were also closely following the situation in Cuba. So we had volunteers to come join us in the expedition!

I've never told this story before. But that's what happened. We came up with a plot to figure out how we were going to return to Cuba, no matter what.

The Soviet people—our teachers, ordinary people—showed a great deal of solidarity with us. They knew about the unilateral decisions taken by the Khrushchev government and were against them. They also knew about Fidel's declaration that the moral missiles we possessed in Cuba were more powerful than the nuclear missiles. All these speeches reached the Soviet people.

Protests in the United States

WATERS: During those same days in October 1962, we were organizing demonstrations in the United States. Jack and I were both university students at that time, in different cities.

LÓPEZ CUBA: You were organizing support activities?

WATERS: Yes. To demand "U.S. Hands Off Cuba!" "U.S. Out of Guantánamo!" "Stop the Invasion!"

BARNES: Communists in the United States had had no contact with revolutionists in Cuba when the crisis began, of course. But we supported the Cuban revolution, wholeheartedly. Some revolutionary-minded young people in the U.S., including myself, were actually won to communism in Cuba. I spent several months here in Cuba in the summer of 1960. I recall asking a Cuban compañero I had come to trust whether he thought I should stay in Cuba or go back to the United States. I wanted to stay, because we all knew the invasion was coming.

"Go back to the United States," he told me, "and make a revolution there."

I decided he was right. And I've never gone back on that agreement.

During the October Crisis there were a few older socialists in the United States who had been worn down by the retreat of the labor movement and the McCarthyite witch-hunt during the 1950s; they held the view that there was nothing much anyone could do. "Either the Russians and the Americans will go to war or they won't," they said. "It's too late to demonstrate; too late to go onto the streets."

We responded, "Well, all we can do is fight. Washington has to know they will pay a price if they go to war against Cuba."

The big majority in the communist movement in the U.S.— young or old—responded as we did. We knew the Cuban people were ready to fight, and we were determined to fight alongside them. The most important lesson for young revolutionists to learn is that the imperialists pause only when they have to face those who are ready to fight like you are in Cuba. Otherwise one starts believing that all of history is negotiated by big governments.

LÓPEZ CUBA: What you say is very important because popular pressure in the United States is what forced the U.S. government to pull its troops out of Vietnam.

The Cuban revolution today remains on a firm footing. At the same time, the U.S. government knows that the progressive people of the United States, the working people, will take to the streets to oppose an attack on Cuba, as they did during Vietnam. There is solidarity with Cuba around the world, as well, and this too has acted as a brake on Washington.

Of course, we continue to be under blockade. During the October Crisis it was a military blockade, but the economic blockade is just as cruel and violent. We will overcome this one too.

Revolution in Nicaragua

WATERS: Elsewhere you've spoken about your experiences in Nicaragua as head of Cuba's military advisers to the Sandinista government. You have explained that it takes a high level of leadership to be able to advise and provide aid, even when not everything is being done the way you would do it. That it is harder to act . . .

LÓPEZ CUBA: . . . as an adviser than to be a combatant. Yes, that is the hardest task.

BARNES: I have been asked by some of our youngest and most fiery comrades: "Why didn't the FAR make them act like the FAR in Nicaragua?" And I tell them that a very important political question was at stake here: Either the Nicaraguan revolution will be made by Nicaraguans, or it will not be made. Another day will come, and the Nicaraguans must look at Cuba as people who always treated them with utter respect and dignity, under the most difficult circumstances.

Clearly, this must have been a very difficult responsibility you shouldered in Nicaragua. There are many young workers and revolutionists in the United States who would like to know: Would you do anything differently if you had it to do over again?

The Nicaraguan and Grenada revolutions were central to the revitalization of our movement in the United States, and they had a similar impact on millions of revolutionary-minded workers and youth in Cuba. So it would be useful for us if you could say a few words about your experiences in Nicaragua, and about the differences between serving as an adviser there and commanding your own forces here in Cuba.

LÓPEZ CUBA: That is a complex question.

Let me begin by going back in time to the defeat of the Batista army, which had U.S. government advisers. To understand how we were able to defeat this army, it is important to look at where the rebel forces that fought Batista came from— to look at our origins as a popular army.

The armed forces across the continent, of course, were prepared to back the existing governments. They were ready to defend the interests of the bourgeoisie and the landlords of their respective countries, as well as the U.S. interests in these countries.

But these armed forces were not prepared for one major contingency—that is, they were not prepared to confront an internal struggle, fought by irregular forces with popular support.

Following the triumph of the revolution in 1959, the U.S. government took a series of measures to ensure that Cuba would not be repeated elsewhere on the continent. The approach of the U.S. government, and accordingly of governments in other countries in the region, began to change in order to prepare these armies for whatever contingency might occur.

In Nicaragua, the Sandinista guerrillas had spent many years fighting heroically to defeat [the dictatorship of Anastasio] Somoza, and we know how many years the guerrillas fought in El Salvador too. The U.S. imperialists gave the reactionary forces in those countries a great deal of support to prevent the triumph of the revolutionary forces.

Following the Nicaraguan revolution, the guerrilla movement that took up arms against the Sandinista regime was not the same in its composition as the one that had done so against the Cuban regime in the Escambray mountains. In the Escambray, those who took up arms were those who wanted to regain their wealth with the support of the United States. They were the ones who joined the invasion force at Girón.[4]

In Nicaragua the situation was unique. It was poor people, people of humble background—supported and equipped by the U.S.—who were actually engaged in fighting the government. This was a government that had declared itself revolutionary, right in the heart of Central America—in a location the United States considered very dangerous, since the revolution's influence could spread both north and south. The North Americans were willing to spend their last dime in Nicaragua to make sure the Sandinistas failed.

This was the situation we faced. We had supported the Sandinista guerrillas before the triumph in 1979, and we re-

4 For more on the struggle against counterrevolutionary bands in the Escambray see the interview with José Ramón Fernández, pages 108–14.

sponded immediately to the request to advise and to assist
the new government. But the Nicaraguans were the ones who
would decide—that was always our conception. They were
the ones who would defend their revolution. We could not
interfere in their decisions, nor take positions that would undermine their authority.

That is how we functioned during the ten, almost eleven
years we were in Nicaragua—with a great deal of tact, a great
deal of care, a great deal of respect.

The government confronted a very difficult situation. The
war was a protracted one. It was taking a cruel toll on the
people, and on their children. The external pressures on the
Sandinistas were very powerful, and they saw a way out
through elections.

We tried to convince them that under those circumstances
of war, elections were not the correct way to resolve the problems they faced. We knew that imperialism was going to throw
all its economic power into the balance around those elections. Owing to Nicaragua's extreme poverty, it would have
been very difficult for the Sandinistas to have won more votes
than the opposition, which was supported by reaction and by
foreign capital. We foresaw what the outcome was likely to
be. But the decision was one the Nicaraguans had to make.[5]

Draft army or volunteers?

The Sandinistas had both Cuban and Soviet military advisers, and we didn't always agree on our advice. The Soviets
argued for a large, professional, technically sophisticated, regular army. We, on the other hand, believed Nicaragua needed
an army capable of eliminating the irregular forces they confronted internally, and that this could not be accomplished by

---

5 The Sandinista National Liberation Front, which had led the workers and
peasants in taking power in the 1979 revolution, scheduled elections to a
National Assembly for February 1990. The FSLN was defeated in those elections by a bloc of bourgeois parties and employer and landlord organizations.

a regular army. These differences over the conception of the struggle and structure of the army were ones we also faced in Angola and elsewhere in Africa.

An irregular struggle, we pointed out, had to be fought with irregular forces prepared for such a struggle, not with large regular units. It had to be fought by volunteers. That's how we defeated the bandits in the early years of the Cuban revolution.

Under difficult and complex conditions such as those in Nicaragua at the time, it isn't easy to draft a soldier, put him under discipline, and take him to war. Given the country's poverty, a soldier called up to serve often had to leave his family in hunger. And the war, which had begun barely a year after the Sandinista triumph, dragged on for eight or nine years.

There were brave and excellent soldiers, excellent combatants—on both sides. They were all Nicaraguans, with different ideals, different interests. It was a cruel struggle, one that bled the Nicaraguan people.

That's the situation we found ourselves in the middle of, as we sought to aid the Sandinista government during the more than ten years it existed. All of us are aware of the outcome, but I believe they made a big effort to preserve the revolution.

Today Nicaragua is suffering the consequences of a neoliberal government. During the years of the revolution, Sandinismo registered some gains for the exploited classes, for the peasants and workers, but all this is being dismantled today. The government is taking away the land from the peasants, and nationalized properties are being liquidated. That is the situation in Nicaragua today—a sad one, but the reality.

WATERS: Many of us spent time in Nicaragua during the years of the revolution, and the *Militant* and *Perspectiva Mundial* maintained a news bureau there for more than a decade, beginning within weeks after the victory in July 1979. We followed the revolution closely. I remember what happened when the Sandinistas decided in 1983 to institute compulsory military service, rather than continuing to build an army based on politically motivated volunteers. The landlord-capitalist opposition and their sponsors in Washington immediately launched a political campaign to turn layers of the toilers against the revolution.

LÓPEZ CUBA: The enemy and other reactionary forces in Nicaragua exploited the issue of the draft, demanding that it be eliminated. I think this was a decisive factor in the outcome.

The conditions existed to create a volunteer army without the need for conscription, since Sandinismo had the support of broad popular forces in Nicaragua. Due to the conception of the need for a large regular army to fight an external enemy, however, they continued applying the military service law in order to achieve such professional military structures.

In fact, the first units of the Sandinista People's Army in the opening years were trained in irregular warfare and composed of volunteers. They could have eliminated the counterrevolution with volunteer forces—without the need for a draft army.

Political education in army

WATERS: The young generation here in Cuba does not have opportunities right now to participate in internationalist missions of the kind that your generation and others have had. Such missions have provided not only essential military experience but have been a central element of political education as well. Could you talk a little about political education and training within the armed forces today?

LÓPEZ CUBA: The political work in the armed forces has a very rich history. It goes back to our war of independence against Spain, and later to the irregular war against Batista. Many cadres and leaders of the revolution received their fundamental political education in the *guerrilla* in the mountains.

During the period since the triumph of the revolution, it has been the aggressive policy of the United States itself—its unrelenting pressure—that has been the biggest stimulus to political and ideological work among the combatants and the people. To underline this point, I'll remind you that early this year we decided to hold our congress[6] in the midst of the tense, difficult, and complex economic conditions created by the U.S. blockade.

By chance, Che's remains were found in Bolivia just a few months after the party congress had been called. It's incredible what it has meant to bring back Che's remains—as well as those of the compañeros who fell with him in combat— right in the midst of our preparations for the congress, and then the congress itself. And you saw the ceremonies giving posthumous tribute to Che and his compañeros, and laying their remains to rest in Santa Clara.[7] It's incredible to see the effect this has had on the political morale and consciousness of our people.

Ever since the triumph of the revolution, there have been particular events that have strengthened the unity of the people and the leadership of our country. During the early years, for example, there were all the threats we confronted and repelled with our small Rebel Army, reinforced by the volunteer militias. There was the fight against the bandits in the Escambray, Girón, the October Crisis. In 1964 we faced a crisis when the U.S. Navy seized some Cuban fishermen and

6 The Fifth Congress of the Communist Party of Cuba opened in Havana on October 8, 1997—the thirtieth anniversary of Ernesto Che Guevara's capture in Bolivia and murder at the hands of his captors the following day.

7 Che Guevara's remains were found in Bolivia in July 1997, together with those of six other revolutionary combatants from Bolivia, Cuba, and Peru. All were killed in the course of the 1966–67 guerrilla campaign led by Guevara to topple the military dictatorship in Bolivia and link up with rising revolutionary struggles elsewhere in Latin America, especially in the Southern Cone. The remains of the seven combatants were brought back to Cuba, where hundreds of thousands of Cuban workers and youth mobilized to pay tribute to their example and to express determination to remain true to that revolutionary course. On October 17, in a solemn ceremony in Santa Clara, the remains were placed in a monument built to honor the combatants.

our government cut off the water supply to the Guantánamo naval base.[8]

Not a year has passed without threats, I believe. And that fact, of course, makes it necessary for the military and political cadres of the revolution to base ourselves on the population. There's no other way to have confronted what we've lived through over the past thirty-eight years. We've had to work hard; we've had to carry out political work with the combatants, with the militias, with the people. And all this has forged greater unity among the people.

There's no question, as you pointed out, that our internationalist missions have been a catalyst for the values that exist among the Cuban people. Being willing to fight for Cuba is one thing. But it's quite another thing to say: let's go to Angola, let's go to Ethiopia, let's go to Nicaragua, let's go to Mozambique, let's go to Syria.

When I was in Syria I was sometimes asked: "How many dollars did they give you to come here?" The same question was sometimes asked when I was in Angola, and in Nicaragua. And I would reply that I received nothing. "We are not mercenaries," I would say. "My salary is given to my family in Cuba, and they are provided with what they need. I don't need anything here."

This is something very difficult for anybody in a capitalist army to understand, of course. But it also gives an insight into the qualities of our people and armed forces.

During the war in Nicaragua we decided to send teachers there, and thirty thousand Cubans volunteered to take part in this internationalist mission. Two of these teachers were killed by the contras, and within a few hours of learning about these murders one hundred thousand of our people volunteered to go.

8 On February 3, 1964, the U.S. Navy seized four Cuban fishing boats with thirty-eight crew members. In response, the Cuban government cut off the water supply to the U.S. naval base at Guantánamo. The fishermen were released two weeks later.

That's the way it is in Cuba. Throughout difficult years, the people have been on the side of the revolution. And this has been the foundation upon which we have organized political and ideological work within the armed forces.

Impact of economic measures

There is no question that the economic measures we've had to take in recent years—the agricultural markets, self-employment, the Basic Units of Cooperative Production (UBPCs), the decriminalization of the use of hard currency—represent a big challenge for us today.[9] These measures undoubtedly transform consciousness somewhat, particularly in the new generations. Because among those called up to serve in the armed forces today may be the son of a self-employed person, the son of a UBPC member, the son of someone who receives money from relatives living in the United States.

So, we've had to refine and improve our political education work in light of this reality. What is our starting point? We start from the fact that after the triumph of the revolution, right up until 1967, we had self-employed people, we had a farmers' market. In other words, all the things we've now had to reintroduce out of economic necessity have existed before in the history of the revolution. But the sons and daughters from all those social layers took part in internationalist missions.

During the fight against Batista, there were people who sold their photographic equipment or their carpentry shop to raise funds to buy arms for the July 26 Movement. Later on, during the first years of the revolution, people left their jobs or gave up their businesses to go to the Escambray to fight the bandits. Others closed up their shops and went to Girón to repel the invaders—just like that, in an instant! They simply closed their doors and went. Later, after they had returned, some of these

9 These measures have been adopted since 1993 as a consequence of the severe economic conditions in Cuba, known as the Special Period (see glossary notes).

people were mobilized—for months at a time, in some cases—and meanwhile their shops remained closed. I'm talking here about people who made their living through those shops.

In other words, our experience shows that all popular sectors can be patriots and fight for the revolution. This is where our great task lies. You can be a self-employed person and also be a communist and a revolutionary. You can receive money from your family in the United States and also be a patriot—that is, also be someone who fights on the side of the revolution.

It's true that a Cuban who gets $25 or $30 sent from the United States has the equivalent of the monthly wage I receive as a general. That's a mathematical fact, if you look at the exchange rate between the dollar and the peso. Our real wage, of course, is not just our paycheck of 500 or 600 pesos. We also receive benefits such as education, health care, social welfare. All sorts of things that would be very expensive in any other country—housing, for example; schools; telephone bills—are very inexpensive in Cuba. We receive all these things as a result of the revolution, but they are not included in our wage.

Cubans today who work in a mixed enterprise, or who have jobs related to tourism, receive benefits that the rest of the population do not. This is the challenge we confront today in political and ideological work, I believe. We face it in the armed forces—because we get young people in the FAR who are under all these influences—but also more broadly in Cuba as a whole. During the recent party congress, the commander in chief pointed out that in face of these challenges we must not overlook the kind of political work that has to be carried out every day.

The youth is the sector of our society where many of these influences I've been describing are the greatest. So while we don't have any internationalist missions today, we must involve young people in the big effort to pull the economy of our country out of the Special Period. And this, of course, involves a great deal of political and ideological work.

The documents of the recent party congress are now being

studied not only by all 770,000 members of the party and half million members of the Union of Young Communists, but also by the combatants in the armed forces and the rest of the population. Nothing about the congress is a secret. Everything will be accessible to the people, so they know what was discussed, how it was discussed, and what they can do to help get out of the difficult situation we still face.

Throughout this forty-year historic process in Cuba, the armed forces have relied on patriotism and motivation to keep our troops at a high level of morale and combat readiness. This is at the heart of our work. In carrying it out, we have the great advantage that despite their age—the commander is seventy-one and the minister is sixty-six—Fidel and Raúl have great vitality. They are our best political workers. They have a direct rapport with the troops through their speeches. The minister is constantly visiting the units and talking with individual soldiers, as well as with the leadership of the party and of the Union of Young Communists in the armed forces. The commander works directly through his own intervention, as well as through written instructions.

It's important that we have a minister of the armed forces, Raúl, who is very demanding in the training and political education of our troops. This helps us a great deal in carrying out our responsibilities for political and ideological work in the armed forces.

That is what I can tell you. This was a difficult and complicated question, but an interesting one nonetheless, since it's something the enemies of the revolution understand very little about. Isn't that right? Many of them were predicting that we would collapse when the Soviet Union and the socialist camp disappeared, but the truth is that we are not going to disappear.

Why Washington targets Raúl

BARNES: What you've just said about Raúl is particularly useful for us, since he has long been a special target of scurrilous propaganda in the United States. Raúl is portrayed as a brutal person.

Those of us who have been able to follow the Cuban revolution from the beginning recognize this deception for what it is. But the U.S. press and politicians keep hammering on this theme, as one of the ways they try to undermine support for the Cuban revolution among new layers of workers and young people. We'd appreciate anything you could say to help us be more effective in telling the truth about Raúl and other Cuban leaders.

LÓPEZ CUBA: Yes, the image they present of Raúl is of an unfeeling person, an authoritarian person. Unfortunately they know little of his virtues: his simplicity, his humanity, his concern for the individual, for his subordinates, for his family, for the people.

This false image is more and more being broken, I believe. But the enemies of the revolution still exploit it.

You will notice that when Fidel refers to Raúl, he doesn't talk about him as "my brother." No, he says Raúl is second secretary of the party because he has *earned* that responsibility during the years of the revolution.

The world needs to become better acquainted with Raúl's qualities as a leader, as a man, as a human being, as a person of feeling. That's undoubtedly true.

BARNES: It's very difficult to be a commander in a revolutionary army. You must make decisions that affect people's lives, so you have to be objective. Friendship can have nothing to do with it. As you're making those decisions, however, a revolutionary commander cares deeply about every single soldier and his or her family.

LÓPEZ CUBA: That's true.

BARNES: But officers in capitalist armies are not like that, so they don't understand these leadership qualities you've been describing. At the same time, these are qualities that revolutionary-minded fighters in mass work and in the trade unions in the United States deeply admire in the FAR. They look to it as a revolutionary institution that produces the kind of leaders they seek to emulate. That's why what you say about Raúl is important for reasons above and beyond setting the record straight.

Washington lives on the hope there will be a division in the FAR and in the party leadership in Cuba. But they don't understand the FAR. They confuse their hopes with reality.

LÓPEZ CUBA: Yes, that's true. This is an old wish of theirs. When Che left Cuba in 1965, the enemies of the revolution began speculating about disagreements between Che and Fidel. These stories began circulating before Fidel made public Che's farewell letter to him a few months later in 1965, but they've continued ever since. There is no more convincing explanation as to why Che left, however, than that letter to Fidel. It is extremely valuable as a political testament.[10]

Land mines: 'Weapon of the poor'

WATERS: An interesting interview appeared in *Granma International* a few weeks ago with Cuban brigadier general Luis Pérez Róspide, who heads up military industries for the Revolutionary Armed Forces.[11] The interviewer paraphrases Pérez Róspide as saying that his department of the FAR has the "basic mission of guaranteeing that each Cuban has a rifle, a land mine, and a grenade to defend the country."

The article continues, noting that when the general was asked about the manufacture and utilization of land mines, which are opposed by some rich countries, Pérez Róspide "gave his opinion that no one discussed this issue with the poor or those who are threatened by nuclear weapons and have none of their own. 'Land mines are the weapon of the poor,' General Pérez Róspide declared."

10 Che Guevara's farewell letter addressed to Fidel Castro, written before he left Cuba for the Congo, was made public in October 1965, at the meeting where the Central Committee of the Communist Party of Cuba was presented for the first time.

11 An interview with Brig. Gen. Luis Pérez Róspide, director of the Union of Military Industries, was published in *Granma International*, September 28, 1997.

We'd like to get your opinion on this question, since a very big campaign is under way in the capitalist world, promoted by the governments of Canada and various members of the European Union, to sign an international treaty banning land mines.

LÓPEZ CUBA: Yes, and unfortunately this campaign also has broad backing among persons who are very progressive, very humanitarian, and who have enormous respect in world public opinion. To some extent this is understandable, since this is a very human question.

But one has to ask: What about the two flights by B-29s that dropped atomic bombs on Hiroshima and Nagasaki? How many people were killed? How many victims are still dying from the effects? If a nuclear arsenal exists capable of annihilating the world, why not fight against this?

Because mines are the weapon of the poor. They are the weapon of those who don't have the resources to buy a B-52 bomber or an F-16 fighter jet.

A number of years ago, when the collapse of socialism had already begun, the Soviets gave us a final squadron of MIG-29 fighters. Six were delivered.

Recently, the Russian government proposed to sell the FAR more of these MIG-29s. The minister asked them: "How much do they cost?"

"Twenty million dollars," he was told.

So the minister replied: "We'll sell you back the six we already have!"

Actually, we have been making an effort to sell these MIG-29s, and to get authorization from the Russians to collect payment. Because a poor country like Cuba, whose armed forces and budget depend on our economic possibilities, cannot afford these expensive aircraft. We cannot afford other types of expensive and sophisticated weaponry, nor are they particularly necessary if we take into account the popular character and strictly defensive purpose of our weapons, including the antipersonnel mines we have, which are not for use in another country.

So what can we use to resist? Weapons that are the least

expensive—rifles, mines, Molotov cocktails, antitank grenades. That is why we have to adopt this stance against banning land mines.

How many billions of dollars does the United States sell in arms to Third World governments? It's an incredible figure—and at the cost of hunger, of dire poverty. How many millions are killed by the "bombs" of starvation, lack of electric power, health care, food? And why does this happen? Because of the dependency of these countries on big capital. Because of the exploitation of the people of those countries. That's the truth.

Yet they single out mines to be against—because they are weapons of the poor. If we had our way, we would rather not have mines, or rifles, or any other weapons. Let them respect the sovereignty of the peoples. Let there be justice. But as long as we continue to be under constant threat, we are the ones who are accountable for the security of our people.

That is why we have been very cautious in giving our opinion on this world campaign against mines.

We know all about land mines. The majority of the combatants we lost in internationalist missions were due to mines. The majority of those crippled were due to mines. We know the effects of this weapon. But isn't that true of all weapons? In any case, there are weapons that are much more deadly than mines.

That's the reality. That is the reason for our position.

BARNES: It's when the peoples give up their right to defend themselves that they will be slaughtered.

LÓPEZ CUBA: Yes, that's the truth.

BARNES: People sometimes ask us, "Do you really believe the Americans will use their nuclear weapons someday?" We reply, "They've already used them! Against the peoples of Hiroshima and Nagasaki." And it is only the readiness of people around the world to fight that stops the U.S. rulers from using those weapons of mass destruction once again.

LÓPEZ CUBA: Exactly.

BARNES: So that gives us time to fight to take their arms away from them. American workers will come to understand this very well.

Bay of Pigs

WATERS: We would be very interested if you would talk about your experiences as a tank commander during the mercenary invasion at the Bay of Pigs.

LÓPEZ CUBA: The propaganda campaign in the United States—by Cubans living there, as well as by other reactionary forces—created an impression that an invasion of Cuba would have the support of the entire people, who were against the revolution. This would make it easier for the United States to support the mercenary brigades and later, of course, would facilitate the coming to power of a provisional government and the occupation of Cuba.

Instead, from the moment the mercenaries landed, they were met by machine-gun fire that lasted right up until the invasion was crushed seventy-two hours later. So the North Americans discovered very early the truth behind the lie they themselves had been promoting—that the Cuban people dislike the revolution. From that time on, and especially following the mobilization during the October Crisis, they knew the Cuban people were willing to fight.

The top U.S. leadership is well aware of the price of an invasion of Cuba. That is what has saved us from drastic measures by them.

There was a risk they might have become emboldened as a result of the disappearance of the Soviet Union and the socialist camp. That could have led them to believe that our armed forces might lose their fighting capacity.

That is precisely why we have taken important steps to make sure they know the truth. The truth is that at the time of Girón, half a million people were armed. Today three million people are armed—all the people—and ready to defend the revolution. *The entire people.*

This is what has prevented U.S. aggression from taking on an armed character, I believe. Instead they have chosen two other routes, track one and track two,[12] that start with economic warfare and then move on to ideological confrontation. These are our two real enemies.

WATERS: During the intense period of training shortly before Playa Girón, your first tank units were being formed. In another interview you described how everything you and other combatants learned from Soviet instructors in the morning you taught to the others later that same day.

LÓPEZ CUBA: Yes, we were still basically a guerrilla army when we had to begin confronting U.S. aggression. At the time of Girón, the units of the future armed forces had not yet been formed. The tank crews, artillerymen, and antiaircraft units had not yet completed their training courses. Our pilots were still flying the broken-down old planes inherited from Batista's air force. Most of the weapons and equipment we had purchased to outfit the new armed forces had not yet arrived. In short, we faced a situation that was very dangerous for the revolution.

It was the revolutionary enthusiasm of the people that made the difference at Girón. Our brigades were made up not only of troops, but also of volunteers who just showed up. They knew Fidel was there, and the fact that the commander in chief was present throughout the entire battle had an enormous impact. He was very insistent, very hardheaded. When we wouldn't let him get into one of our tanks, he got in a tank in another column coming from the other direction.

---

12 These are terms often used to describe provisions of the so-called Cuban Democracy Act, also called the Torricelli law, after New Jersey liberal Democratic congressman Robert Torricelli, enacted by Washington in 1992. "Track one" refers to the tightening of the U.S. economic embargo, while "track two" refers to provisions that—in the guise of promoting the "free flow of ideas" between the United States and Cuba—aim to corrupt and buy off Cuban academics and professionals.

We were accustomed to this, since it had been the same in the Sierra. Later, during Hurricane Flora it was the same. During the October Crisis it was the same. Whatever the situation—an assault on the revolution, a natural disaster—the commander in chief was always there at the side of the people who were threatened.

The same was true August 5.[13] He has always been in the front trench, without fear of the risks. That is one of the reasons the revolution still lives, I believe.

FAR's leadership role

BARNES: Following the crisis in the Revolutionary Armed Forces and Ministry of the Interior in 1989, involving Ochoa and Abrantes and several others, many in the United States and elsewhere noticed that the FAR took on even more leadership responsibility throughout Cuba. The breadth of what the armed forces were responsible for seemed to expand. The revolutionary integrity exemplified by the FAR seemed to take on even greater importance. I wondered if you could comment on whether or not this perception is an accurate one? Because those habits and values of revolutionary honor and discipline set a very important example for workers and youth

---

13 On August 5, 1994, a group of some twenty Cubans tried to hijack a boat in Havana harbor to go to Florida. There had been four previous boat hijackings that month, including one a day earlier in which hijackers killed a young Cuban police officer.

The August 5 hijacking was repelled by dock workers and the police in Havana. Later that day a crowd of several hundred gathered along the Malecón, Havana's oceanfront boulevard, throwing rocks and bottles at police, hotels, and other targets. Several thousand workers and youth, supporters of the revolution, poured into the streets to respond to the provocation, effectively quelling the riot. They were joined on foot by President Fidel Castro.

Two days later, on August 7, half a million Cubans paid their last respects to the slain police officer and demonstrated their support for the revolution in the streets of Havana. Every year since then, August 5 has been celebrated by mass demonstrations and other events reaffirming the determination of the Cuban people to defend their revolution.

in the United States and elsewhere.

LÓPEZ CUBA: Yes, that's accurate, if one looks at this from
the standpoint of moral authority and prestige—without this
diminishing in any way the FAR's subordination to the party,
to the constitution, and to the authorities democratically
elected by our people. And the leadership qualities of Raúl
that we were discussing earlier also had a big influence here,
I believe.

Since the triumph of the revolution, there has never been an
economic battle, there has never been a natural disaster, where
the armed forces have not been at the side of the people. Over
thirty-eight years of revolution, there has never been a moment
when the armed forces have not fought shoulder to shoulder
with the people: whether in social efforts, economic tasks, or
defense. This gives the FAR a great deal of authority.

Moreover, we have never allowed corruption in the armed
forces. We are intransigent: the armed forces must be kept
free of all personal interest. This is also an important aspect of
the education of the cadres.

In capitalist countries, I believe, it is not unusual for an army
officer to engage in business, to have capital, and he often
devotes more time to business than to the armed forces. In
the FAR no one is going to find any officer involved in activities beyond the revolutionary tasks we have taken on and the
principles we have established.

In the 1980s, although the armed forces were very professional and technically proficient, we had some gaps in the
areas of administration, finances, and production. So, in 1990
the minister called on the FAR to address these problems.

Raúl has demanded four things from the cadres of the armed
forces. First, they must be political cadres, with high political,
ideological, and moral qualities. Second, they must be highly
skilled military professionals. Third, they must have the basic
skills of food production and agriculture. And fourth, they
must have a rudimentary knowledge of economic affairs. They
don't need to be economists, but they do need to know where

each peso we spend comes from, and how to use it effectively.

We have integrated these requirements into the professional training of our cadres—both of older officers such as myself, and of the youngest ones. This is part of the program of study for new officers, and the veteran officers are given regular refresher courses on techniques of leadership, planning, economics, and production.

An army of workers and peasants

All this gives the armed forces in Cuba more authority, more prestige. I think the origins of our Revolutionary Armed Forces and of its cadres has a lot to do with this, as well. It's no secret to anyone that there are not many Colin Powells who can make it to the rank he achieved in the United States. Because generally the officers in capitalist armies are the sons of the bourgeoisie, of generals, of high officials, of better-off families.

In our army we make sure that our officer corps includes farmers, workers, those from the ranks of the humble, from the masses. Without such a policy, the social composition of the officer corps will slowly be transformed, and in the end will have negative results.

We pay conscious attention to the social background of those who go to officers' school—the Camilitos.[14] Fifty percent of the Camilitos must be the children of workers and farmers. The other 50 percent is made up of children of teachers, doctors, officials, and others. But it's a requirement that half must be from families of workers and farmers, so the army does not lose its class origins.

In spite of spending forty years in the struggle, for example, I continue to think like a peasant, like someone who tills the soil. I have not lost sight of my origins.

BARNES: When your brothers tried to grab you at the time of the triumph and take you back to the farm, you didn't

14 Students at the Camilo Cienfuegos Military School.

know then that thirty-eight years later you'd still be in the revolutionary army. But you are!

On a related subject, in the United States, when officers retire—they're often still relatively young—they are immediately hired by big corporations as advisers and board members, and are given bourgeois salaries and stock options. What's the situation of retired officers here in Cuba?

LÓPEZ CUBA: Our officers retire quite a bit older than in the United States, although we've been forced to retire people at a younger age in recent years due to the economic difficulties we've faced. Because of our concern to maintain the reputation of the armed forces and in line with a strict sense of equality, retired officers, along with all other retired citizens, are not allowed to take jobs in the mixed enterprises, which are jointly owned by Cuban entities and foreign capitalist investors.

Nonetheless, an officer who is fifty, with thirty or more years of active service behind him, still has fifteen years of working life ahead of him. There is room for improvement in this area, since these are people who are highly disciplined, highly trained, very trustworthy and patriotic. We could take better advantage of these compañeros for the benefit of society; they could be more productive in retirement.

Cuba's internationalism

BARNES: When we return home following these interviews, I'm confident we can tell young fighters in the United States—as we have been doing for many years—that when revolutions occur once again anywhere in the world, Cubans will respond to calls for solidarity by organizing internationalist volunteers. The same people who carried out internationalist missions yesterday are leading in the efforts to overcome the difficulties of the Special Period today. And the cadres being trained in the Special Period will be part of the internationalist missions still to come.

LÓPEZ CUBA: By no means have we renounced internationalism. It remains a fundamental ethical principle of the revolution.

The most important internationalist mission we have is right here. That mission is to show the enemies of the revolution that we are capable of developing ourselves, of improving the economy, of bettering the living conditions of the people.

This is the most strategic task we face right now. And all of us who are conscious of its importance need to be a part of accomplishing that task.

'War of the entire people is the foundation of our defense'

DIVISION GENERAL ENRIQUE CARRERAS

MARY-ALICE WATERS/MILITANT

Top: Div. Gen. Enrique Carreras during interview.

Bottom: Carreras standing beside Cuban air force Sea Fury, around 1961.

GRANMA

Enrique Carreras

ENRIQUE CARRERAS, a division general of the Revolutionary Armed Forces, born in 1922, is considered the father of revolutionary Cuba's air force.

A military officer before the revolution, Carreras was trained as a pilot in the United States during the Second World War and after. He opposed the U.S.-backed coup of Fulgencio Batista in 1952 and became a collaborator within the armed forces of the July 26 Movement, led by Fidel Castro, which was fighting the dictatorship. In September 1957 the head of the air force ordered Carreras to bomb rebellious army units in the city of Cienfuegos. He and several others refused to carry out the order, for which they were arrested, court-martialed, and jailed. Carreras was sent to prison on the Isle of Pines, today the Isle of Youth.

After the revolution's triumph at the opening of 1959, Carreras joined the effort to build the armed forces of the new revolutionary government. He was assigned by Fidel Castro to train a corps of pilots.

In April 1961, at the Bay of Pigs, the day they were preparing for arrived. As a prelude to the U.S.-backed invasion, the air force bases in San Antonio de los Baños, Santiago de Cuba, and Ciudad Libertad in Havana were bombed on April 15 by CIA-trained counterrevolutionaries flying planes whose markings had been painted to appear to be those of the Revolutionary Armed Forces (FAR). Seven people were killed and fifty-three wounded. Cuba's few existing planes had been dispersed on Castro's instructions. Only two were destroyed.

The following day, at a mass rally to honor the victims of the attack and to mobilize the entire population for the coming war, Fidel Castro proclaimed for the first time the socialist character of the Cuban revolution.

Expecting an invasion at any moment, the commander in chief ordered Carreras and the other pilots to remain by their planes at all times. They slept on the runway beneath the wings of their aircraft.

On April 17, at 4:45 A.M., Carreras was urgently called to the telephone. Fidel Castro was on the line. A mercenary army was invading Cuba at Girón Beach on the Bay of Pigs. Castro issued immediate orders:

"Carreras, there's a landing taking place at Playa Girón. Take off right away and get there before dawn. Sink the ships transporting the troops and don't let them get away. Understood?"

"Understood, commander."

Over the next seventy-two hours, the air squadron Carreras headed, consisting of ten pilots and eight dilapidated planes inherited from the armed forces of the dictatorship, was decisive in defeating the U.S.-organized invasion. The Cuban planes brought down nine B-26 bombers flown by the counterrevolutionaries and U.S. pilots, sank a number of their ships, and hounded the mercenary troops on the ground. Carreras himself shot down two aircraft, and the fighter plane he was flying was hit twice by enemy fire. Two Cuban pilots and several crew members were killed in the battle.

In subsequent years, Carreras served on various internationalist missions, among them a commission to Vietnam in 1969 to study its antiaircraft defenses. From April to August 1976, Carreras was part of a delegation led by Cuban defense minister Raúl Castro that went to Angola to help organize the Cuban volunteer forces there. Twelve years later, in March 1988, during the battle of Cuito Cuanavale, Carreras was part of the massive Cuban effort that helped Angola repel another South African offensive and sealed the fate of the failed South

African attempt to topple the Angolan regime.

In recognition of his decades-long distinguished record, in 1989 Enrique Carreras was awarded the status of Hero of the Republic of Cuba, the country's highest honor.

The interview with Carreras was conducted in Havana, Cuba, on October 24, 1997, by Jack Barnes, Mary-Alice Waters, and Martín Koppel.

'War of the entire people is the foundation of our defense'

MARY-ALICE WATERS: Your story is especially interesting because you began your political activities while an officer in the old army.

The Socialist Workers Party has always acted on the lessons we learned from Lenin and the Bolsheviks—the importance of carrying on political work within the army, among workers and farmers in uniform. That was our course during World War II, the Korean War, and the Vietnam War. During Vietnam, we argued against those in the antiwar movement who wanted to target the soldiers in the U.S. army as if they were the enemy, even to the point of sometimes labeling all of them "murderers."

Instead, we fought for the anti–Vietnam War movement to organize the types of demonstrations and other actions that would attract GIs, not repel them. The central slogan we advocated, and which eventually became the main banner of the antiwar movement, was "Bring the Troops Home Now!" Our comrades, when they were drafted like hundreds of thousands of their generation, didn't refuse to be inducted. We organized to defend soldiers who exercised their democratic right to march and speak out against the war, when not on active duty. Broad forces in the United States were won to this perspective over time, and antiwar GIs and Vietnam veterans became a growing—and politically very important— force in the fight against Washington's murderous assault on the Vietnamese people. Their contributions very much strengthened the Black and Chicano struggles in those years as well.

For these reasons, among many others, our readers in the United States would be interested to learn how you became a revolutionary.

ENRIQUE CARRERAS: I served in the Cuban armed forces from 1942 until 1957, so I know what military life is. I reached the rank of major.

I joined during World War II, when the government established the Emergency Military Service. I was a student at the time. I enlisted to learn how to use a rifle, and because I wanted to fly.

I came from a family of modest means. My father had been a sergeant in the army. He always told me not to join up, that I wouldn't like it. My mother was a nurse, and she wanted me to become a doctor. What I had in mind, however, was a pair of wings. I had my heart set on flying. I dreamed of being a pilot some day, but it seemed an impossible dream.

It was the war, unfortunately, that allowed me to do it. That's how I got into the military aviation academy. Within a year I had become a pilot.

I was in the service here in Cuba, patrolling the coasts, searching for German submarines that were sinking ships carrying sugar to Europe and on stopovers to or from South America. Several Cuban ships had been sunk, along with ships from the United States and other countries. That was the patrol duty I was doing at first.

In 1944, I was sent to Kelly Field in San Antonio, Texas, to learn to fly a new type of plane. We had been flying the AT-6 and then the AT-11 trainers, and now we learned to fly the B-25 bomber. The 201st Mexican Squadron was also there.

I had a lot of trouble with English in those courses. All I had learned in Cuba was the English they taught in high school, and that wasn't enough. I learned to say "ham and eggs," so

I didn't have any problem with breakfast. But at lunchtime I would ask for breakfast again, and they wouldn't give it to me. Anyway, it was rough.

In the course of World War II, while in the United States, I observed many things. For example, I had never before seen women occupying posts previously held only by men, or training alongside men. At the time of the war there was still a lot of machismo in Cuba. We did not want to see women in the streets alone going to the store, much less working outside the home, even in the fields. The revolution has been eliminating all that machismo.

At Kelly Field I saw women training as pilots and gunners for ferrying B-25 bombers from bases in the United States to Canada, and sometimes even to Britain.

That was my first experience in the United States. What I learned there—the training I received as a combat pilot—I subsequently taught to the pilots we trained in the early years of the revolution, including those who fought at Girón. The same tactics the U.S.-organized forces used in attacking Cuba, we applied against them. But we were defending a just cause, while they were coming to reconquer what they had lost. So we're not talking about moral equivalents.

When the war ended in 1945, in Cuba we started flying not only combat aircraft but also transport planes. I flew mainly in the United States. In the early 1950s I went through a series of basic and advanced combat courses for wing command officers at the Air University at Maxwell Air Force Base in Montgomery, Alabama. I practiced my English quite a bit during that period, too. I completed those courses in 1955 and returned to Cuba.

But by that time, the political situation in Cuba was very bad. In March 1952 Batista had seized power in a military coup.

On July 26, 1953, the Moncada army garrison was attacked. This assault was the motor that drove the revolution forward, even though it failed militarily. The attackers were not able to take the garrison, distribute arms to the people, and open the offensive against Batista—which is what they intended to do. Some of the combatants were murdered right there in the Moncada on Batista's orders. Others were convicted and sent to prison, serving their sentences on the Isle of Pines.

I was in Montgomery at the time of the attack, and I didn't know anything about what had happened until I read it in the newspaper. Another student at the Air University, an officer in the U.S. armed forces, spoke Spanish; he was married to a woman of Cuban descent. He took me to Tampa, where his wife's family lived, and that's where I saw a newspaper report that "a group of communists" had attacked the Moncada garrison. Right from the start they claimed it was communists. I held on to that newspaper for years.

Like a number of other soldiers and officers in the armed forces, I was opposed to the Batista dictatorship. On September 5, 1957, a small naval post in Cienfuegos rose up in arms,[1] and I was ordered to bomb the city. A group of pilots in the squadron I commanded agreed among ourselves to instead drop the bombs into the water. There was supposed to have been an uprising in Havana at the same time, but it didn't happen for a number of reasons.

In prison at Isle of Pines

In any event, my participation in the revolution begins at this point. The conspiracy was discovered, and I was arrested, tortured, court-martialed, and dishonorably discharged by the tyranny. They initially asked for the death penalty. I served time in various prisons, including La Cabaña. Then they sent me to the Isle of Pines, where I began to get to know the revolutionaries who were imprisoned there.

JACK BARNES: You got to know the July 26 people there?

CARRERAS: Yes, compañeros from the July 26 Movement who

---

1 See glossary notes, Cienfuegos uprising.

had come on the *Granma* were imprisoned there. Young people from the Revolutionary Directorate and people from the Popular Socialist Party were also there. All of them were there together.

The political views I held at that time came from the army. Anticommunism and hatred for the Soviet Union had been drummed into my head. That's what they taught us in the academies. I didn't know what a communist was, but everything I had heard about them was bad. I was influenced by all that propaganda.

While serving time in prison, however, I got to know all of them—[Jesús] Chucho Montané and other compañeros from the *Granma*; Lionel Soto; the compañeros from the Directorate.

By the time the revolution triumphed, I was no longer the anticommunist I had been before. I had become a progressive, a revolutionary. And then I witnessed all the acts of aggression organized by the U.S. government in the early years. I came to understand how wrong everything they taught me had been. I learned in the course of the struggle, and that's the best way.

Today I am a Communist Party member, and have been since 1965 when the party was founded. I have attended the five congresses, and I feel happy to be a Marxist, a Leninist, a Fidelista.

October Crisis

BARNES: You said you were deeply affected by the aggression carried out by Washington against the Cuban revolution during its opening years. This month is the thirty-fifth anniversary of the October Crisis. Where were you during these events? How do you recall them?

CARRERAS: The October Crisis was a continuation of the U.S. fiasco at Girón. The defeat they suffered there led them to risk an atomic war. Girón was like a bone sticking in their throats, something they don't accept to this day. In war one either wins or loses. But they can't admit having lost in their efforts to dominate such a small country. If they hadn't failed at Girón, there would never have been an October Crisis.

We don't hate North Americans. We only hate the governments in Washington that have attempted to destroy our revolution. If the Cuban people want this revolution, why does the U.S. government seek to impose its will on us by force of arms? By economic aggression? By acts of sabotage? All these attacks against us began even before Girón.

We were not the ones who provoked the October Crisis. They did—by breaking relations with Cuba, by preparing a mercenary brigade, and an invasion. They are afraid of Cuba. They are afraid the example of our revolution could spread. But how can we be blamed for doing things well?

BARNES: You can't be convicted for setting a good example!

CARRERAS: That's right, we can't. We're not the problem, but rather our neighbors who won't accept that we've freely chosen socialism. We are not a military power, or a threat to anybody. We are a small island. They know we are not capable of attacking them, that we have no intention of doing so.

On the other hand, if they set foot on Cuban soil, they will have to pay an enormous price.

BARNES: In the United States they are now publishing for the first time the transcripts of the meetings in Kennedy's offices during the October Crisis. They confirm what has been reported before, but it is amazing to "hear" it all unfold meeting after meeting.

In the early days of the crisis Kennedy had decided to invade. The reasons are interesting; they discuss their options in these meetings. They thought that if they bombed the missile sites they would kill a lot of Russians, and that might lead to nuclear war with Russia. If they took military action to enforce the blockade and stop the Russian ships on the high seas, heading for Cuba, the first shots would be against Russian forces, again raising the risk of nuclear war.

So the political chiefs decided invasion was the way to go. The fighting would be primarily between Cubans and the U.S. military, they reasoned, and given U.S. military superiority it would be over fast, the risk of nuclear confrontation less.

Then Kennedy asks the Joint Chiefs of Staff for an estimate. "What will be our casualties?" Because Kennedy is a politician. He's not a military man or a dictator. He needs to weigh the political consequences.

He gets the answer. Expect 18,000 casualties in the first ten days. That's more casualties than they ended up suffering between 1960 and 1965 in Vietnam!

From that point on in the transcripts, discussion of the invasion option recedes. The political chiefs begin in earnest to search for other alternatives.

Even today you often read articles in the United States arguing that the Cubans wanted a nuclear war but Kennedy and Khrushchev found a way out. The truth is very different, however; only the strength and determination of the Cuban people prevented war, prevented a nuclear holocaust.

We use the example of Cuba to explain why if you want to prevent nuclear war you have to follow a revolutionary course. The imperialist rulers have to know they will face what they faced in Cuba in October 1962, what they have faced in Cuba for almost forty years.

CARRERAS: Today, I'm convinced the number of casualties would be double what Kennedy was told back in 1962. Today, even more so than at that time, the Cuban army is truly the entire people.

Anyway, you asked what I was doing during the October Crisis. I was the representative of the air force at the command post of the commander in chief. Captain Flavio Bravo was the chief of operations.

We experienced some very difficult moments in our meetings, especially when flights by U.S. reconnaissance aircraft nearly provoked war. RF-101 reconnaissance planes were flying 300 meters above our bases, photographing all our equipment. Fidel said, "No more!" He gave the order to open fire on any plane that came within range of our weapons.

And they were indeed *our* weapons.

The Soviet weapons were not under our command. Only the Soviet officers could order that they be fired, and only upon orders from the Soviet Union. We didn't have the authority to tell them, "Bring down those planes." But Fidel did give the order to open fire on reconnaissance planes that came within range of our own antiaircraft defenses.

At that time we had only a small air force. Some MIG-19 interceptors. Some 100-millimeter artillery, those with the longest range. Some *cuatro bocas*, 37-millimeter guns with four barrels. That was it. But when morale is high, you defend the country with whatever weapons you have. Violation of our air space was a grave offense against our sovereignty. And when we fired the initial shots at the first squadron of planes that came, we chased them back. That was the end of the RF-101s.

Downing of U-2 spy plane

Then Washington sent in the U-2 planes—planes that flew so high our weapons couldn't reach them. That's when the Soviet officer who commanded the antiaircraft battery in Holguín gave the order to shoot down a U-2.[2] I recall watching the radar screen in the command post as the U-2 went down.

I was a captain at the time, and was responsible for maintaining coordination with the Soviet air force. They had a squadron of forty MIG-21 interceptors, as well as a squadron of IL-28s that transported land mines, torpedoes, and other

2 A U.S. U-2 spy plane was downed over Cuba on October 27, 1962. Contrary to instructions from the Soviet high command in Moscow, and without requesting permission to fire, a Soviet officer ordered his troops to launch antiaircraft missiles that brought down the plane violating Cuban air space.

weapons. There was great friendship and cooperation among us in face of the threats. Nobody was doing anything crazy. The ones doing crazy things were Kennedy and the Pentagon, so the Soviet officer did what we would have done and took action against the u-2.

The u-2 had been piloted by Major Rudolf Anderson, who was killed. I saw the body. I know that when there is one death others follow—that's how wars start. With the downing of the u-2 we thought the war had begun. The opposite happened, however. They decided to hold talks.

The Soviets took part in those talks, along with the U.S. government. But we were left out. Had we known what was happening, we wouldn't have stood for it, but as it was we had no choice. We didn't agree to the outcome, but we had to accept it.

If the October Crisis had not ended as it did, we would not be going through what we are going through today. I don't know if I've made myself clear. Our situation today is the consequence of that situation. [3]

BARNES: Washington knew how to deal with the Soviet leadership; they knew how to get agreements from them. They always remember the 1939 Soviet-German pact that brought World War II closer.[4] But the U.S. rulers don't understand Cuba. They think you are like Moscow, like Eastern Europe, only a special tropical variety. They don't know you're the opposite, that a Soviet-German pact would be impossible with Cuba.

---

3 Commenting on the outcome of the October Crisis in a 1992 NBC television interview with Maria Shriver, Cuban president Fidel Castro said: "Naturally we did not want war. We wanted a solution, but an honorable solution. . . . We didn't know that the crisis was on its way to being resolved on the basis of the almost unconditional concessions made by Khrushchev. They left everything the way it was. They left the blockade. They left a dirty war. They left Guantánamo Naval Base."

4 See glossary notes, Soviet-German pact.

The truth is, they may not understand you but they fear Cuba like nothing since the Russian revolution. And they will never leave you alone as long as you remain the kind of example you are—one where there has never been a gap between word and deed.

When we interviewed Div. Gen. López Cuba earlier this week, he told us about the impact Cuban soldiers training in the Soviet Union during the October Crisis had on their instructors and other ordinary Russians. What about here in Cuba itself? Did you see changes among the Russian soldiers and officers, influenced by the courage of the Cuban people? Were they ready to fight alongside you if Washington decided to come?

CARRERAS: The Soviets had a problem with their high command in Cuba, because their officers here felt the same way we did. They faced the same situation we did. In an atomic war, all of us were going to be wiped out. All the Cubans said goodbye to our children. We'd see who was alive when it was over. War was coming. October 27—the day the u-2 was shot down—is a date I'll never forget. I'm telling you, the thing was for real.

At the beginning of the crisis, the Russians thought nothing would come of it. But that wasn't our view. And within the command structure of the Soviet forces here many were upset with the orders they were getting from home. Their hands were tied: they had a general staff here, but the orders were coming from the Soviet Union. The general staff here didn't agree with letting U.S. planes fly reconnaissance missions over Cuba.

I'll give you an example. It is one that was never reported here, but it is part of the history of the October Crisis that you are putting together. A squadron of Soviet planes was flying from Camagüey to Havana, and by chance they came across some American planes. They had those planes in their gunsights, and requested authorization from their high command at home to shoot them down. The high command over there in the Soviet Union said no. Those Soviet pilots returned to base utterly demoralized.

The pilots' conflicts were not with us; they were with the Soviet high command back home. And the differences were deeply felt. Those pilots were here in Cuba, thousands of kilometers from the USSR. It was their lives that were on the line.

The decision to shoot down the U-2 was not the result of an order from Moscow. It was the individual decision of the head of the Soviet antiaircraft defense in Oriente province.

'Brothers to the Rescue' raid

We still face these kinds of dangers today. The enemies of the revolution have kept on violating Cuban air space, and if they continue doing so—whoever does it—we're going to be back to the October Crisis some day. And while Cuba does not have atomic bombs, we do have the moral bomb of a people who won't put up with tyranny.

That's why the two planes that violated our air space were shot down in 1996.[5] For months those planes had been flying over Havana and elsewhere, dropping leaflets against the revolution. Measures had to be taken. That group of extreme

---

5 On February 24, 1996, three Cessna planes organized by the Florida-based counterrevolutionary organization Brothers to the Rescue were warned several times that they had entered Cuban air space. Two were shot down, and four men on board were killed. Cuba had experienced ten other violations of its air space within the previous twenty months, involving some thirty planes all told. On at least three occasions the planes scattered leaflets from the air. The same organization mounted flotillas to violate Cuban waters several times during this period. In response to these aggressive acts, the Cuban government, in a statement published in *Granma International*, July 26, 1995, publicly reaffirmed its long-standing policy that "any vessel coming from abroad, which forcefully invades our sovereign waters, could be sunk; and any plane shot down. . . . We have confronted this provocation with great patience, but patience has its limits. The responsibility for whatever happens will fall, exclusively, on those who encourage, plan, execute, or tolerate these acts of piracy."

right-wing Cubans who have gone to Miami were violating our air space. To this day, they are making preparations to attack us. And they receive support. They are allowed to carry out these violations.

We're not going to let them, however. So another crisis could occur. It might not be in October; it could be some other month. But they need to stop and think. They need to take steps to avoid a confrontation that we don't want, and I don't think they want either. They should just leave us alone and let us work. But they've got that bone stuck in their throats.

BARNES: When those planes were shot down in February 1996, the *Militant* and *Perspectiva Mundial* retold the story of the October Crisis, to help workers and youth in the United States and elsewhere around the world understand why Cuba had to say no to violations of its sovereignty. A front-page statement by the National Committee of the Socialist Workers Party explained that this decisive action by the Cuban government slowed down Washington's aggressive course and was a blow by Cuba against war. If Cuba allowed that kind of violation of its air space to occur, we explained, then the next probe would come, and then the next, and then the next— and at some point there would be war.

It's Cuba's resistance that prevents a war, as it has for almost four decades. That's a very important lesson for working people in the United States to understand.

CARRERAS: At the end of the last century, we fought against the Spanish colonial power to free ourselves. The U.S. government intervened at the end of our war of independence to advance its own policy of expansionism, going to war against Spain in 1898. What did the U.S. forces do when that war ended?[6] They forbade Cubans from marching together with

6 At the conclusion of that war, Washington took direct possession from Madrid of Puerto Rico, the Philippines, and Guam as U.S. colonies, while imposing the Platt Amendment on the Cuban government established during the U.S.

them as victors. They didn't even let our *mambises* enter Santiago de Cuba. Everything the U.S. forces did, from the very start of their invasion of Cuba, was aimed at creating conditions to destroy the entire *mambí* army.

We are the continuators of that *mambí* army and its traditions. They sacrificed themselves for Cuba's freedom then, just as we are willing to sacrifice ourselves today.

I mentioned earlier that I had taken courses in the 1950s at the Air University in Montgomery. Some of my teachers there used to ask me why Latin Americans and Cubans are so rebellious—you seem to go from one revolution to another, these teachers would say. I explained to them that hunger and necessity force people to change, and that change means revolution.

For the past thirty-eight years or so I would add something else: that to this day, there has been no more worthwhile course for the popular masses than socialism. That is why we in Cuba—starting with our leader Fidel—say "Socialism or death!"

Raúl Castro

BARNES: We want to ask you about the minister of the armed forces, Raúl Castro. We posed a similar question earlier this week to General López Cuba.

Raúl is singled out for vilification by the U.S. rulers and their media, in some ways more so even than Fidel. To me it is very strange, because I spent three months in Cuba in the summer and fall of 1960 and got to know a little about the commanders of the revolution, how they were viewed by the people of Cuba. Raúl had a reputation for being, among other

---

military occupation. Under the provisions of that amendment—incorporated in Cuba's new constitution—Washington asserted the "right" to intervene in Cuban affairs at any time and to establish military bases on Cuban soil. These provisions were eliminated from the Cuban constitution in the wake of the 1933–34 revolutionary uprising there.

things, one of the warmest of the commanders. I came to the conclusion that they try to demonize Raúl because they fear the continuity of leadership of the Cuban revolution. They also fear the army, of course, and the armed people of Cuba. Raúl becomes a target because, next to Fidel, he is the long-time commander of those armed forces.

So, let me ask you as well: What kind of man is the minister? Why do you think the enemies of the revolution attack him in the ways they do?

CARRERAS: I didn't know Raúl or Fidel personally at the time of the triumph of the revolution. Nevertheless, I did know about them through the political activity they had carried out, going all the way back to Fidel's years as a student leader at the University of Havana in the late 1940s, and then Raúl's student days in the early 1950s after the Batista coup. I knew them through the actions they took at Moncada, and the *Granma* landing. They chose the line of armed struggle to overthrow the tyranny. There was no other way. They were the ones who saw it, who did it.

That's how I began to get to know Raúl and Fidel, well before I had ever met them. Fidel reached Havana a few days after the revolution triumphed, and Raúl came somewhat later, and we got to know each other there.

Personal relations between the minister and myself grew as time went on. As a flight instructor I really applied myself so he would learn to fly well. He was indefatigable, and very young. I must have been about thirty-six years old then; he was still in his twenties. That is how we began to get to know each other. In the air and on the ground. To tell you the truth, I learned a lot from the example he set.

Raúl is a very capable man, very well trained militarily, brave, and decisive. He has helped make the Revolutionary Armed Forces the vanguard of the revolution. Fidel has always had confidence in the leadership of the FAR, its organization, and its training.

If the enemies of the revolution attack Raúl, it's because he is a great commander of a great army, an army of the entire people. He *is* very human. He always asks about my family—the children, the grandchildren. In his personal traits, he's very much a Cuban. He has a great affinity with the masses.

Of course, we don't want nature to take Fidel away from us, since he is, as they say, the star that shines the brightest in the Cuban revolution—and, for that matter, in the Latin American revolution, too. That's why our enemies attack Raúl—because they know that with him, we'll have no problems if something happens to Fidel. But there won't be a problem with anybody else, either. We have a large number of very well trained officers.

Unfortunately, however, the enemy has a big propaganda apparatus, which it uses for external consumption. Here, they can say what they want; it does not have much of an effect on anyone.

Fidel and Raúl have the best qualities you'll find in a leader. What's unusual is that two such individuals emerged, prepared to take any risk and to head a mission as difficult as the one we are carrying out.

You look at them and sometimes you ask yourself, "Where did they learn so much?" Perhaps the priests really know how to teach, because that is where they both studied![7]

Revolutionary integrity and responsibility

BARNES: I remember watching some television coverage from Cuba in 1989 of various proceedings during the crisis involving Ochoa and the Ministry of the Interior. You could see in Raúl's face how deeply he had been affected by this breakdown of revolutionary integrity among even a handful of officers in the FAR and Interior Ministry.

In following these events, it seemed to us that as part of

---

7 Like most children from middle-class families in prerevolutionary Cuba, both Fidel Castro and Raúl Castro were educated at church schools. The Belén School they attended was run by the Jesuits.

Fidel's response to this crisis, he turned to the FAR to shoulder even more responsibility and take broader political initiative to guarantee the direction and honor of the revolutionary government. That also seemed involved in the decision to appoint Furry [Gen. Abelardo Colomé Ibarra] to replace Abrantes as head of the Ministry of the Interior. How did the Cuban people see these developments?

CARRERAS: The Cuban people entrusted the continuity of the revolution to Fidel and Raúl. And we can say today that there are cadres here in Cuba capable of carrying forward that continuity who were not even born when Fidel and Raúl were already engaging in struggle.

The struggle itself is a school in which you learn things you can't learn in regular schools. You learn how to fight. You learn how to confront problems, and how *not* to confront problems. Imagine sullying our uniform for money, to get out of an economic bind! That's what Ochoa did. And this in an army as honorable as the Rebel Army! If we have to die of hunger we'll die of hunger, but we won't disgrace what the people have fought for so hard and so long. We won't disgrace what so many people have died for over the years. We must honor those who have fallen.

What was done by Ochoa and those involved with him is incompatible with the principles we defend. Anyone who violates those principles knows the consequences. We regretted having to shoot someone who had once been a revolutionary. But a revolutionary cannot stain his hands, or take the wrong road in order to obtain funds for things our people need. Here there can be no contraband, no drugs. *Not here.*

If once again we are seeing prostitution—the problem of the so-called *jineteras*—that has come with the growth of tourism, it is something we are combating. I look at my little grandchildren, and while I don't want anything bad to happen to anyone, I see things first through my family. In my family, in reality, I recognize my people.

That's why we fought for socialism—to eliminate such evils.

Look at what's happening in Russia today. Look at what's happening in Romania. Look at what's happening in all those European countries. We will not permit those evils in Cuba.

Recently a code of ethics was approved in our country reaffirming the necessity for a high moral standard among cadres, and that code is being applied. Such standards are essential if the people are to support the leadership and cadres of the revolution, because the population is small—11 million—and very alert. People see how you live. We don't have to point out abuses, because the people do so and begin fighting the cadres implicated.

Raúl has been very vigilant, not only as a general of the army but as the second secretary of the Communist Party. He has always sought to guard the honor of the party, the example set by its members.

So, this effort by the enemy to vilify Raúl is for consumption abroad—it won't work in Cuba. They don't know the Cuban revolution.

Vietnam and Cuba

WATERS: You were in Vietnam for several months in 1969. Could you tell us about that?

CARRERAS: I was in Vietnam, although not as a combatant. I was there for several months as part of a commission to learn from the experiences of North Vietnam's antiaircraft defenses against the U.S. bombing. The commission included radar specialists, communications experts, and so on. We saw how the tiny Vietnamese air force was organized, and learned how they were often able to use the radar guidance system on incoming enemy planes to determine targets in advance and minimize the effectiveness of U.S. air strikes.

We traveled from Hanoi down close to the border with South Vietnam. The Vietnamese didn't let us go further, since several other members of our commission had already been killed as a result of taking big risks. These compañeros, who had arrived in Vietnam earlier than I did, found themselves

in the middle of an antiaircraft battery under attack. A U.S.
Navy plane had launched a missile against a radar installation, I believe, and the Cubans tried to take cover and watch
what was happening at the same time. The missiles hit and
exploded, killing them.

The Vietnamese didn't want the same thing to happen to
us. They never wanted anybody to fight alongside them. They
did want cooperation and aid. And they shared their experiences with us, since sooner or later we too were likely to be
subjected to the same kind of aggression. We relayed these
experiences back here to Cuba. It was extremely useful in training our pilots and preparing our antiaircraft defenses, so that
air strikes against us would be less effective.

We saw firsthand the criminal character of the U.S. bomb-
ings. The U.S. warplanes destroyed all the bridges. They attacked cities using fragmentation bombs. Women and children
would go into their homemade shelters—lengths of pipeline
buried underground. Sometimes, however, they couldn't shel-
ter themselves adequately, and children were killed when clus-
ter bombs hit the ground and fragmented. We saw these things
happen. It was a criminal war against the Vietnamese people.

We learned from these experiences and changed our own
defensive tactics. The truth is that the enemy compelled us to
keep making these changes—and continues to do so now that
we are alone, now that we no longer get the aid we used to
before the socialist camp, in Fidel's words, fell like a meringue.
It just disintegrated.

The war of the entire people—that is the foundation of our
tactics and strategy. We are ready to confront whatever attack the enemy might carry out against us. You've been here.
You've learned something about our ground troops. And we're
preparing as best we can to make sure that the air force is
never destroyed. The majority of our aircraft are in underground shelters; others are above ground but in reinforced
shelters. Even so, of course, we all know that U.S. weapons
are very sophisticated and dangerous, and that no matter what

measures we take the air force is going to suffer greatly. That's
why our strategy has always been based on making clear that
any country that invades this island will pay a very high price.

Invading Cuba would be a very big risk for them. Cuba and
the United States are very nearby, so it would be a lot harder
for them to hide the consequences of the war. It would be a
lot easier for people in the United States to see things close-
up in Cuba than they were able to do in Vietnam—and, despite that, your antiwar movement won out. The closer to
home events are, the faster your movement can win.

Let's hope they never get so crazy over there as to come
here to attack us. We don't want deaths. All we want is to be
able to work. All we want is to be able to help humanity,
especially in Latin America, which is going through very painful
times right now. There is a lot of hunger, a lot of poverty. And
only revolution, only social change can salvage the situation.
Today, children are paying a price for something they haven't
done—for things adults have done.

Here in Cuba we are fighting, we are resisting.

Special Period

BARNES: How has the Special Period affected the armed
forces and its responsibilities?

CARRERAS: The Special Period has had a big impact, defi-
nitely. There's a lot to say about that.

You are aware, for example, that we have virtually no oil
deposits in Cuba, and the little we do have is not very good
quality. It has high sulfur content. This fuel shortage keeps us
from maintaining our armed forces in optimal condition.

Prior to the breakup of the Soviet Union, the Soviet government sold us large quantities of oil, and we paid very low
prices. The end of these shipments was very abrupt. We had
no time to make adjustments. Suddenly no one could find even
a liter of oil. But we had maintained a strategic reserve, and
that saved the day. Fidel and Raúl had always insisted on that
for defense purposes. We ended up having to utilize part of

the strategic reserve so the lights could stay on, so refrigerators could function, so hospitals had electricity.

As the economic situation worsened, we kept on learning. The party leadership guided this effort. We have been learning the appropriate measures to tackle the difficulties we face. We've had to change our defensive strategy, for example. We've had to cut back the armed forces and relocate many cadres to agriculture, to tourism, to study other fields. We've had to keep reducing the air force, which is the most expensive part of the armed forces.

What is our plan? Conservation of resources—so that when the time comes, when the combat alarm sounds, we have what we need. So that our planes can fly. So we can use our artillery. We have tanks and other weapons stored away, much of it underground, some above ground. The above-ground weaponry is for use in the event of a surprise attack, to provide time to put the rest into service.

With the onset of the Special Period, our armed forces budget was cut in half to begin with, reducing it by billions of pesos. Then we cut it again. Now, we're making further reductions in compliance with decisions of the fifth party congress earlier this month.

Who has made it possible for us to make these adjustments without affecting our defense preparedness? The people. The people are organized in the Territorial Troop Militia and in the reserves, as well as in the standing army.

The standing army is the part that is best equipped technically. For example, our air force has combat-ready air units that can respond immediately to attacks, giving us time to activate the people and the aircraft being kept in reserve. Some combat pilots remain on active duty and continue their normal schedule of flying time, while others fly for reduced amounts of time. Reserve units are kept ready for use, and there are pilots flying transport planes who can be called up when the combat alarm goes off or a state of alert is called. We maintain flight crews and a minimum of training. Each active-duty pilot flies between one hundred and two hundred hours during the course of a year. The reserve forces fly a maximum of ten hours a year.

Thus, as needed, we can and will mobilize the same air force we had before the Special Period.

We remain combat-ready, twenty-four hours a day. Nobody flies over Cuba without authorization. Our radar units not only help with air navigation, but inform us immediately of any object that appears in our skies. As soon as the radio message comes in, the fighter planes take off.

That's what happened in 1996 with the planes from Florida we were discussing earlier. We let them come close and then told them several times to turn back. They didn't want to cooperate, however, so down they went.

So, yes, the Special Period has had an impact. We generals like to have large units, but we can't afford that pleasure right now. We have put many planes and a lot of artillery into reserve. But faced with a state of war, they would be reactivated in order to mount a rapid response.

'The war for beans'

We are waging a war in Cuba today, but it's an economic war. It's the war for beans, as Raúl says.[8] And it's more difficult than a shooting war.

The war for beans is the one we're fighting right now. When

8 In an August 3, 1994, speech to the National Assembly of People's Power, Raúl Castro said: "Today, as our commander in chief has just pointed out, the central strategic, economic, political, ideological, and military task for all Cuban revolutionaries, without exception, is to guarantee the population's food supply, and to produce sugar, as Fidel has consistently pointed out in recent times.

"Yesterday we were saying that beans are as important as guns; today we are affirming that beans are more valuable than guns, using beans generically to cover all indispensable basic foods. (However, so as not to confuse the United States; we do have guns and other weapons in plentiful supply for the defense of our country.)"

the pilots are not flying, they are planting some of those beans, or harvesting them. They go to the farms and help out in agricultural tasks. Those on active duty rotate with those in the reserves. They keep in good shape, physically and medically. They set an example for other compañeros.

As a revolutionary, I'm still learning, even at my age. I was never a farmer, and I used to dislike working the land. But when I sit at the table and eat rice, plantains, and beans, I have to ask: "Where does it come from?" It comes from the land. I'm not a good farmer, but when we go to the farms, I do my part. I want the young people to see the old-timers take part in bringing in the beans.

We have felt the cutbacks very much. But we are content. The Revolutionary Armed Forces does not have advisers of any kind. We are our own advisers. That's what I'm doing now: I am an adviser in the Ministry of the Armed Forces. They ask me about the early years, how we did things back then. I respond as best I can, and that is a great stimulus for me.

I can assure you that the young generation is better prepared than we were—politically, intellectually, culturally, in every sense. That's what the majority of the new ministers who were just chosen are demonstrating. That's the generation that is replacing us.

BARNES: In the United States we tell revolutionary-minded workers and young people that the living traditions of the Cuban armed forces represent for us today what the young fighters in the soldiers' soviets in Russia meant for toilers the world over in 1917. It has the same kind of political attraction to revolutionists as the army Lenin and the Bolsheviks forged seventy years ago to defend the young Soviet workers and peasants republic against the counterrevolutionary bandits of that time, and against the invading imperialist armies that backed them.

Right now, the FAR is the only revolutionary army working

people and youth in the United States today have a chance to see. And they need to learn about and understand a revolutionary army, because some day they are going to be soldiers in such an army.

No worker in the United States has ever known a general like those in the Revolutionary Armed Forces of Cuba. Young workers who've served in the U.S. army know the officer corps as a caste who consider the ranks to be trash—just pieces of meat to be trained, used, and disposed of, dead or alive. That is one of the reasons the generals of the FAR who spoke to the young people from the Americas taking part in the youth festival last summer had such a tremendous impact on them.[9] Young fighters in the United States had the opportunity to learn about some very important history, the traditions of a revolutionary army.

Many revolutionary-minded workers in the United States study the Russian revolution, and they develop a pretty good feel for the workers' soviets—the mass councils of workers' delegates that grew up in the heat of battle and formed the foundation of the new revolutionary government. Workers and other young people in the United States even develop somewhat of an understanding of the peasants' soviets, although fewer and fewer of them today have ever been on a farm. But they have a much harder time understanding the soldiers' soviets, since it's even a step or so further removed from anything they've ever experienced, even indirectly. So we tell them: learn what you can about the armed forces in Cuba, and you'll

9 During the 14th World Festival of Youth and Students in Havana in July–August 1997, many delegates participated in a meeting with four generals of Cuba's Revolutionary Armed Forces who had fought with Ernesto Che Guevara during the revolutionary war against Batista and during internationalist missions in the Congo and Bolivia. The officers were Division General Ramón Pardo Guerra and Brigadier Generals Harry Villegas Tamayo, Enrique Acevedo González, and Luis Alfonso Zayas. The meeting, attended by some 1,500 delegates, was held at the conclusion of a two-day anti-imperialist tribunal during the festival.

have about as good a feel for the soldiers' soviets as is possible short of major new revolutionary developments.

Traditions of Cuban army

CARRERAS: If you'll pardon my saying so, armies have their own traditions. The Soviets have theirs, of course, very strong ones. We have our own traditions—very appealing ones, which we fight to maintain and guard.

Who were our soldiers in Cuba's war of independence from Spain? The slaves, the peasants—that's who joined up as soldiers together with Carlos Manuel de Céspedes to liberate Cuba and put an end to slavery. During the revolutionary war against Batista, the majority of the soldiers who joined the Rebel Army were peasants, as well as workers and students. That's the source of our traditions. And you can't transfer experiences from one country to another.

I've seen firsthand the traditions of other armies, traditions very different from our own. For one thing, we are incapable of laying a hand on a soldier. That is the greatest abomination we can imagine. Yet once, right in front of several of us, I witnessed a Soviet general strike a soldier for being drunk. I can put up with a lot, but seeing that made me so angry I had to get out of there. Laying a hand on a soldier shows a lack of respect, and that's something we do not allow. That's just the way we are.

BARNES: Yes, and your traditions are more like those of the young working-class and peasant soldiers in the soviets of 1917 who gave everything when Lenin and the Bolsheviks called on them to defeat the imperialist invasion and the counterrevolutionary armies of the landlords and capitalists. That is what we have always believed.

The example of Che is part of your traditions, too, and this month, October—here in Cuba, in the United States, and elsewhere—we've been commemorating the thirtieth anniversary of the combat waged in Bolivia by Che Guevara and his comrades. For Che the military, the political, and the economic were not separate, unconnected arenas, but instead parts of an integrated strategy to fundamentally transform society and in the process transform the human beings engaged in that revolutionary activity. Could you tell us a little more about what Che's example means for the cadres and leaders of the Revolutionary Armed Forces, and for the Cuban people?

Che Guevara

CARRERAS: Che is the greatest exponent of the Latin American revolution. As Fidel explained in Santa Clara last week, few individuals have done what Che did to point the way for humanity—to give everything, as he did.

I flew with Che a number of times. I got to know his personality. Che foresaw and spoke about many of the things that are happening to us in Cuba today. He was a man of great foresight, like Fidel—who has even greater foresight. Both of them were able to see things far down the road, and that proved decisive in helping us emerge victorious from the most difficult moments the revolution has passed through.

The image of Che can be found wherever there is a young person who wants to change humanity. Che does not represent only armed struggle, only Cuba, only Argentina. No, he represents the image of the new man.

This is why the enemies of the revolution criticize Che so much. Because his example continues to threaten them. But here in Cuba, we have worked hard to bring Che forward again. And now we have him here among us.

BARNES: It seems important for us to explain in the United States that a Peruvian and a Bolivian family decided they wanted the remains of their loved ones to be buried in Cuba alongside Che's. That was a free decision by the families of these combatants.

At a public send-off meeting in Chicago for this trip at which Mary-Alice and I spoke just the day before coming here, a comrade asked me: "So that's their final resting place?" I said I didn't know. There will be a revolution in Peru some day, and a revolution in Bolivia too. So, "final" is probably not the word we are looking for.

We had supper last night with a friend here in Havana who has never been a member of the Communist Party. "I never march in the May Day demonstrations here," she told us. "I've never liked big crowds." It's a lie when the press in the United States says people in Cuba are forced to go out in the streets, she told us. "I almost never go." But there have been two times, she said, when she did go out. The first time was when U.S.-backed counterrevolutionaries blew up the Cubana plane in Barbados.[10] And the second time was earlier this month when the military procession for Che came through her neighborhood en route to Santa Clara. "I found myself going down to join everyone else along the road," she said.

That's a very important story to tell in the United States, I think. Because it's another piece of evidence that if the U.S. rulers ever invade Cuba, they won't just be fighting the FAR; they won't just be fighting the Communist Party; they truly will be fighting the Cuban people.

WATERS: Is it accurate that you taught Che to fly?

CARRERAS: Yes, that's partially true. Che started out flying with a compañero who had been in his column in the Rebel Army. He had been a crop-duster pilot. This compañero—his name was Orestes Acosta—died in the air attack on our bases that preceded the invasion at Girón. So Che came to me and said, "Carreras, why don't you teach me aerial acrobatics?" He loved acrobatics.

I'll tell you an anecdote. Whenever I fly, whether as a pilot or an instructor, I'm always careful about safety measures—and even more so when I had Che in the plane.

But Che always had a cigar in his mouth. He loved cigars.

---

10 On October 6, 1976, Cuban counterrevolutionaries set off a bomb on a Cubana Airlines flight from Barbados to Cuba. All seventy-three people aboard were killed.

He was a very respected person, and I didn't know quite how to tell him, "Throw away that cigar before you blow us both up!"

So at first I said, "Commander, permit me to hold your cigar while you fly."

"No, Carreras, it's out. The cigar isn't lit."

Then I asked him, "So if it isn't lit, why do you need the cigar in your mouth? I'll hold it for you."

"No, it relieves my asthma."

He had an answer for everything! Imagine! Cigars help your asthma!

He said it so seriously, however, that I let him talk me into keeping the cigar. But whenever he flew with me, I always made sure the cigar wasn't lit. He was the minister of industry and had other major leadership responsibilities. If Che's plane had caught fire, what a price to have paid for a cigar!

My relations with Che were working relations, and we never had much of a chance to talk when we were on the ground. When Che was head of the FAR's Department of Instruction, I was head of the air force and had various working meetings with him to coordinate training on naval and army aircraft. That was when he was also working in INRA [National Institute of Agrarian Reform].[11]

I learned a great deal from Che, and, like many others, deeply regret that he was killed. But Che is not dead. In fact, I believe his presence is being felt more and more in the new generations that are playing a key role in world developments today.

---

11 Beginning in early 1959, Guevara headed the Rebel Army's Department of Instruction, which was responsible for political education in the fast-growing military. *Verde Olivo*, the FAR's magazine, was also "published under the guidance of the Department of Instruction of the Revolutionary Armed Forces." Che was named head of INRA's Department of Industrialization in October 1959.

'The Revolutionary Armed Forces are the people in uniform'

BRIGADIER GENERAL JOSÉ RAMÓN FERNÁNDEZ

Top: José Ramón Fernández at Playa Girón with Fidel Castro, 1961 (Castro and Fernández at center, facing camera).

Bottom: Brig. Gen. José Ramón Fernández during interview.

José Ramón Fernández

José Ramón Fernández was born in Cuba in 1923. As a young military officer, he opposed the U.S.-backed dictatorship of Fulgencio Batista imposed on Cuba through a March 1952 coup. Together with other similarly inclined officers and men, Fernández worked in secrecy to depose the brutal regime. He was part of an unsuccessful revolt on April 4, 1956, by army officers who became popularly known as *"los puros"* (the pure ones). For his participation in that failed attempt, Fernández was arrested, court-martialed, and incarcerated by the Batista regime in the infamous penitentiary on the Isle of Pines. He remained in prison for almost three years.

On the Isle of Pines, Fernández came to know a number of revolutionary-minded fellow prisoners, including members and leaders of the July 26 Movement, and was won to their political perspective. For more than a year he acted as military instructor to these political prisoners, who organized their own battalion within the prison.

On January 1, 1959, news reached the prison of Batista's flight from Cuba in face of the advancing Rebel Army backed by a general strike and growing revolutionary upsurge throughout the country.

The political prisoners demanded immediate release. Hasty consultations ensued between the military commander of the Isle of Pines and high-ranking officers in the capital who were scrambling to pull together a government to replace Batista's in hopes of preventing the Rebel Army from seizing the Havana and Santiago de Cuba garrisons. A few hours later the commander, accompanied by a score of military officers who had been released from detention, flew off to Havana.

Fernández, who was working closely with imprisoned July 26 Movement leader Armando Hart, was among the officers released. He headed not for the airport but for the Isle of Pines garrison, where he ordered the soldiers to lay down their arms, assuring them there would be no persecution of those who had committed no crimes. They obeyed. Then, with four or five soldiers who had never displayed animosity toward the prisoners, Fernández headed to the cellblock. With a machine gun targeting the guard post in front of the entrance, Fernández ordered the gates immediately opened. They were. The July 26 Movement battalion he had trained lined up in disciplined formation and marched out of the prison.

Fernández and Hart, at the head of the battalion, quickly took control of the Isle of Pines, with Fernández its military commander. Forty-eight hours later, he was summoned to Havana.

Rebel Army commander in chief Fidel Castro asked Fernández to head up the school for cadets to train Cuba's new revolutionary armed forces. Fernández replied that he'd already been offered a job as manager of a sugar mill. Asked how much the job paid, Fernández answered 1,000 pesos a month. Castro said the revolutionary government couldn't pay that much.

Fernández argued he didn't feel worthy of the assignment being offered him.

"I think you're right," said Castro, exasperated. "You go off to the sugar mill. I'll go off to write a book. And let the revolution go to hell!"

That day Fernández accepted assignment as director of the school for cadets.

In April 1961, working directly under Castro, Fernández was the field commander at Playa Girón, where the popular militias and Revolutionary Armed Forces defeated the U.S.-

organized Bay of Pigs invasion force in seventy-two hours of combat.

For a decade beginning in 1972, Fernández served as Cuba's minister of education.

No longer on active duty, José Ramón Fernández is a vice president of the executive committee of the Council of Ministers, and is president of the Cuban Olympic Committee. He is a member of the Central Committee of the Communist Party of Cuba, and a deputy to the National Assembly.

The interview with Fernández was conducted in Havana, Cuba, on October 25, 1997, by Jack Barnes, Mary-Alice Waters, and Martín Koppel.

'The Revolutionary Armed Forces are the people in uniform'

MARY-ALICE WATERS: Perhaps we could begin with how you became involved in the struggle against the Batista dictatorship before the revolution, and your responsibilities in building the new revolutionary army once the old regime had been destroyed.

JOSÉ RAMÓN FERNÁNDEZ: I was imprisoned for three years during the struggle against Batista. I had been part of a movement formed in early 1956 by young officers mainly from the military schools and the Havana garrison. We attempted to overthrow Batista and restore the bourgeois democracy that had existed here. Although the scope of the 1940 constitution of the Republic of Cuba was quite advanced, it was never enforced, as you know.

Batista's March 10, 1952, military coup was prepared and organized by a group of active-duty army and navy officers neither whose ideas nor records augured anything good for the country in any way. They were joined by a large group of retired officers who came from the post-1933 years when Batista was the strongman in Cuba, a disgraceful past. The coup was supported by some venal politicians with ties to Batista and his theft and corruption in the previous epochs.

After March 10, there were a good number of officers who had not been able to prevent the coup, but did not accept it

nevertheless. Small groups of conspirators spontaneously began to develop. They were sometimes diverted by the ebb
and flow of promises that, from time to time, appeared to
offer a political solution to the conditions Batista's coup had
created in the republic.

As time went on, however, it became clear that no political
solution was possible, that Batista would enact no change or
reform that would benefit the people. With the sole aim of
personal enrichment, he arrogantly and intransigently held
on to power. As opposition grew, the regime became crueler
and more bloodthirsty.

After the electoral farce of 1954, which sought to legalize the
position of Batista, he was formally inaugurated as president
in early 1955. The small groups that had arisen spontaneously
started to coalesce. On April 4, 1956, a military movement,
which the people referred to as *"los puros"*—"the pure ones"—
tried to topple Batista. It failed and a large number of those
involved were sent to prison; others went into exile, retired,
left the army, or were transferred to distant commands. The
measures taken against particular individuals depended on the
extent of one's supposed support to the Batista regime, or the
degree of sympathy one allegedly had with the movement
being born.

When the revolution triumphed, I joined the Rebel Army as
a first lieutenant, the same rank I held previously. Since I was
a trained professional (and I say this with no vanity), I was
given the task of helping to train the Rebel Army—more than
to train it actually, to help transform the Rebel Army and the
Revolutionary Armed Forces in general.

The Rebel Army had a few thousand men who had fought
against the army of Batista's tyranny. Their numbers had
multiplied in the final days of December 1958 and continued multiplying in the first days of January, attracted by
the prestige and authority that the Rebel Army had
achieved through the armed struggle, and by the revolutionary honesty of the guerrilla leaders under the com-

mand of Fidel Castro.

There was great hope that this army would be both the guardian of the revolution and the base of support for the gigantic task that lay ahead to transform the society and its political, economic, and social system; to preserve our sovereignty; and to impose a code of honor and ethics in public affairs. All this, I repeat, gave the Rebel Army popularity, sympathy, and great prestige. Many thousands of young people were attracted toward it, as well as others of all ages, and the revolution really needed that.

This was a very complex period. The Rebel Army, fulfilling the tasks that fell to it by law, was replacing Batista's corrupt army of 80,000 men. It benefited from its reputation as a patriotic army defending the people, a reputation it continues to consolidate today. Both the Rebel Army and the people repudiated the army that had served Batista, an army that committed crimes and abuses right up to the fall of the tyranny.

At the beginning of the period immediately following the triumph of the revolution, there was not, in general, a clear and firm consciousness of the need for structures, for discipline, for the norms indispensable to a modern-day military force. The members of the Rebel Army—although excellent combatants who had been capable of defeating the corrupt army of the Batista tyranny—needed training along these lines. It was essential to organize and train these cadres in the handling of weapons, in tactics, in combat engineering, in communications, and in all those specific areas of knowledge essential for any armed force.

It was a very interesting, a very important process, in which Raúl [Castro], minister of the armed forces since the early days, was decisive. He is a revolutionary with a tremendous sense of organization, discipline, and an understanding of the need for technical training. He is very methodical—very persistent in working continuously on whatever is important for a given task.

'War of the entire people'

As you know, Fidel is commander in chief, a position he has held since the Sierra Maestra. As president of the Council of State, he is also, by law, supreme commander of the armed forces. He lays out the strategic lines. The concept of the war of the entire people is Fidel's, for example; it is the guiding philosophy of our armed forces today. We don't aim to crush an invasion, or an armed attack by whatever great power— I'm not mentioning names—with our armed forces alone. Our armed forces are powerful, but all the people are needed to inflict such a defeat. A defeat like the one suffered by Joseph Bonaparte's army in Spain.[1] A fighting spirit like that of the Vietnamese. The aim is that the adversary, the invader, will see in each citizen an enemy who, through ambushes and continuous attacks, allows no respite; that each citizen makes sure the invaders never feel safe. That's why we say we are unconquerable.

We can arm considerably more than one million people— sufficiently trained and organized. The armed forces have been reduced in numbers in recent years, without sacrificing their combat capability. Our weapons are in good condition and are adequately distributed and protected. Training remains solid, and our reserves keep growing. Morale is high and we are determined to win, as Fidel and Raúl have taught us. Men and women, the entire people, form a shield that makes the revolution invincible.

Fidel and Raúl know, just as you do, that the primary force is the individual human being—a will to fight, a love of country, a sense of honor and duty. To be determined to fight, a man or woman must be convinced of why they're doing so. In our case the people fight to defend a society where there is

---

1   Napoleon Bonaparte's brother Joseph was proclaimed king of Spain in 1808 following France's conquest of that country. A popular war of resistance within Spain laid the basis for the defeat of the French forces, which were finally driven out in 1813.

no racial discrimination; where the role of women has been expanded and continues to grow; where education—I would say an exemplary education—is free and available to the entire people; where there is a public health care system that, despite shortages, maintains a low infant mortality rate and a high life expectancy, and that treats and fights diseases in a way comparable to any economically developed country. A country where there is social security that has left no one destitute, in spite of the economic crisis. A more just society, where those of us who shoulder responsibilities dress, eat, and work the same as the people as a whole, with great modesty; where there are no special food rations or other privileges.

A country with a democracy, where the entire people participate in making important decisions; where the entire people participate, in the most direct way conceivable, in electing those who govern.

A country where we have defended our sovereignty, where love of country and defense of the national flag are paramount and where the first requirement is loyalty to the country, loyalty to the socialist revolution. That is the first requirement, one that cannot be replaced by anything of a technical character.

We live in a world where we deeply need these convictions and practices in order to be able to fight and win.

Participating in a modest way in building the Rebel Army in the early years, as I did, coming to be vice minister of the armed forces with Raúl under the leadership of Fidel, has been the true fulfillment of my life; this is what has given it meaning. The fact that I was able to participate in the armed struggle in defense of the country at Girón has contributed greatly to this personal fulfillment.

Finally, I can say that today the armed forces, at the head of the people and under the leadership of our party, constitute a formidable enemy for any adversary. We are not looking for war with anybody. But whoever attacks us, if he doesn't die, will have to retreat after one, three, five, ten years of fighting us, or our children, or our grandchildren. We defend the sovereignty of the country and socialism. This is what we fight for. This is what we work for unstintingly.

October 1962 Crisis

JACK BARNES: Perhaps we could raise a question about the October Crisis. We are commemorating the thirty-fifth anniversary of those days right now, and understanding the lessons of that crisis is an important question for us in the United States.

FERNÁNDEZ: And a difficult one for me, since I did not participate in it directly.

BARNES: Some of the previously classified documents and tape recordings from the Kennedy administration that have been released over the past few years give new evidence of what communists in the United States have always explained to the American people about the October Crisis. What we said as youth—demonstrating against U.S. government war moves in the streets of Los Angeles, of Chicago, of Minneapolis, and elsewhere—has been confirmed.

As you know, the story as told by most of the capitalist media and politicians in the United States is that U.S. president John Kennedy and Soviet premier Nikita Khrushchev saved the world from nuclear war, in spite of Cuba. We've always said no. It was Cuba, the Cuban people, the FAR that saved the world from nuclear war. Through their courage and determination, they made Kennedy understand there were limits to aggression beyond which his administration would have had to pay too great a price politically.

The Kennedy White House had been stepping up plans to invade Cuba throughout the entire period leading up to the crisis, and it initially seized on deployment of Soviet missiles in Cuba as the pretext to do so. But the documents that are now being published show that when Kennedy asked the Joint Chiefs of Staff for an estimate of the casualties that could be expected from an invasion of Cuba, they responded with the

figure of more than 18,000 dead and wounded American soldiers in just the first ten days! At that moment Kennedy, who
was not a military dictator but simply a politician facing the
American people under conditions of bourgeois democracy,
began looking for other options. It was that estimate of the
armed resistance U.S. forces would face in Cuba that made
Kennedy begin looking to find a way out.

You can now follow all the White House discussions, day
by day, hour by hour, in the transcripts of tape recordings of
meetings in Kennedy's offices. Even better, you can listen to
the tapes themselves at the John F. Kennedy Library in Boston. You can hear the pauses, the inflections that are sometimes more expressive than the words.

We educate young fighters in the United States to understand that revolutionists must study the past in order to be
prepared to act in all situations—and 1962 will not be the last
year that sees an "October Crisis." Times are coming when
the working class will once again confront nuclear or other
forms of blackmail from the capitalist exploiters and war makers, and revolutionists must know how to stand firm and prevent the rulers from wreaking destruction.

When two small planes that took off from Miami were shot
down over Cuban territory in February 1996,[2] we explained
that this did not register some new policy course by Cuba.
The decision had been made and announced to the world by
Fidel many years earlier during the October Crisis. "You cannot violate Cuba's sovereignty," the Cuban people and their
leadership said. "We will stand." And it's very important to
demonstrate that resolve whenever the aggressors begin new
probes.

That's how we try to educate workers and youth in the
United States about the October Crisis. We would appreciate
any thoughts or opinions you have about it.

FERNÁNDEZ: You have said something that is very true: pre-

2 See interview with Carreras, pages 69–70.

pare ourselves well for war, so we can win peace. If we didn't have the military power that we do, we would have been attacked. I have no doubt about that. Girón was an alert, but in more recent years there have been other warning signals. The danger—as attested to not only by attacks and sabotage but by systematic threats and a consistent pattern of hostile acts—has led us to maintain our defense capacity in readiness and to continuously increase and improve it.

At the request of the legitimate government of Angola, Cuban forces fought against an invasion backed by several capitalist powers that had penetrated more than one thousand kilometers into Angolan territory. History will one day recognize that in winning the liberation of Namibia and putting an end to apartheid, an important role was played by the Cuban Revolutionary Armed Forces—which fought in Angola alongside the armed forces of that country, assisting those who had long struggled for such an outcome. We have to say that the decisive victories in the air and on land were won by these troops.

Our forces in Ethiopia,[3] defending that country against Somali intervention, did the same thing as in Angola. It was no accident that our armed forces were capable of fighting and defeating well-organized armies. We are convinced of this and we deeply admire those internationalist combatants who fought in defense of the sovereignty of others.

We maintain a firm position, a principled position. We do not lie, and we always fight and argue armed with the truth. We keep our people informed. This has been an important factor. The Rebel Army in the Sierra Maestra set an example of truthfulness, of ethical conduct, of respect for the integrity of prisoners.

I remember when a U-2 was shot down during the October Crisis.[4] The U-2 was downed because the commander of the Soviet antiaircraft missile forces here, without waiting for in-

3 See interview with López Cuba, pages 24–25.
4 For more on this incident, see interview with Carreras, pages 66–69.

structions from Moscow, complied with the order given to the Cuban antiaircraft batteries, to fire on anything within range of our weapons.

U.S. planes began flying low over various military installations and areas where our troops were positioned. They had been warned that "beginning in the morning we will shoot at anything that flies overhead." When we started to shoot the flights stopped.

In other words, we must have right on our side, and we have to be firm and intelligent in order to defend it. History will one day record that few statesmen in the modern epoch of humanity have had the talent, wisdom, courage, and capacity to take advantage of the opportunities of the moment that Fidel has had in defending the revolution.

For almost forty years we have been navigating along the edge of a possible attack, firmly defending our sovereignty, the revolution, and socialism. And we have maintained a course that has proved capable of defending our principles while avoiding a war.

There is a somewhat defiant billboard in front of the U.S. Interests Section, and it can be read a number of different ways.[5] But I like to view it as saying what we truly feel: That we are not the least bit afraid of you. It shows we are ready to fight. It should not be seen as a provocation, but as a warning: Don't mess with us. We're small but we know how to defend ourselves, and we will defend ourselves. We have the means to do so, we will defend ourselves, and we will win.

I like very much what Comrade Barnes says; I have the same conviction. And I am convinced of something else. For Kennedy it was a political problem not to carry through with the invasion of Cuba in 1961—and I'm not referring just to Kennedy, who inherited the invasion from Eisenhower. It was a political problem because of what those invading forces of Cubans

---

5 The billboard, which faces the building that houses the U.S. diplomatic mission in Havana, says: "Mr. Imperialists, we are not the least bit afraid of you."

armed, trained, and organized by the CIA represented and what they signified in Congress and in different spheres of U.S. political life. It was evident that one sector of the government and the CIA supported the invasion, but it was also clear that an invasion would have had a high political cost because of the number of casualties that the U.S. armed forces could suffer.

But U.S. administrations often understand how bad wars are only when the bodies of dead soldiers start coming back and public opinion starts clamoring. Until the bodies start arriving, war is not bad. It wasn't until body bags started arriving from Vietnam that [U.S. president] Lyndon Johnson began losing sleep, and others started thinking that a solution had to be found. The same thing happened in Korea—we forget about Korea now, but the same thing happened then.

I'm sure the people of the United States would not react the same way if the bodies were coming back from defending against an invasion of Los Angeles, Seattle, Boston, or any other city. But people know and understand when a war is unjust, when the U.S. government is fighting a war outside its territory for hegemony or to advance economic interests.

When I was in a museum in China, I saw on display a statement by Gen. Mark Clark, who had been head of the U.S. Fifth Army in Italy during World War II and later served as commander of the troops in Korea. Following the Korean War, he made a statement that he had the sad honor to sign the peace after the first military defeat of the United States.[6]

The death of every single man hurts us; we take care of every family and every person. We wish no one had to die. But unfortunately we have had thousands of deaths—in the struggle against Batista; in the repression by Batista's forces

6 Clark, who signed the armistice in July 1953 ending the Korean War, wrote in his 1954 memoir that he "had gained the unenviable distinction of being the first United States Army commander in history to sign an armistice without victory."

in the streets of all the cities and in fields across Cuba and in the battles waged by the Rebel Army against the tyranny.

Later we faced the fight against the bandits.[7] I'm sure no one in the United States would deny that these bands were an artificial creation of the CIA, children of the CIA. Just like the grouplets today in Cuba, some of whom seek to present themselves as political parties, often with five people. They receive financial backing from the United States. But those people don't represent anything in Cuba, they're alien to the people. They are the representatives of a foreign power that supports, pays, and maintains them.

Let me make myself clear: I don't mean by this that there are no discontented people in Cuba, or people who disagree with socialism. I'm aware there are—in fact, there have to be. We have shortages, privations, difficulties. We run risks; there are dangers. There are people who are more consumer-oriented, who would like a more comfortable life, without struggles. There are people who perhaps, consciously or unconsciously, place a shirt, a pair of pants, or a car above the country's sovereignty or above social justice, and these people are clearly not enthusiastic about the revolution. That's one thing. But it's something completely different for there to be a sector of the population that has taken organizational form, or that can be given organizational form, that is represented by grouplets such as I described.

These are two different things. These grouplets represent no one, not even themselves, in fact. What they represent perhaps are those who pay them.

Popular support for revolution

We have just held elections.[8] I am the deputy of a municipality in the interior of the country. So I can speak about this

---

7 A reference to the counterrevolutionary bands in the Escambray.
8 Elections to the municipal assemblies of People's Power, Cuba's local government bodies, were held October 19, 1997. In districts where no candidate

process from experience, since I have lived through it and have close ties to my municipality. In the October 19 elections, 97.6 percent of the population voted. I believe Clinton was elected last year by about 50 percent of 50 percent, by approximately 27 percent of the eligible voters in the United States.

Here some ballots are left blank and others are intentionally spoiled; in these elections it came to 7.2 percent of the ballots cast. Some people, particularly those who are very old, vote for two or three candidates when they're only supposed to vote for one, for example. Others intentionally vote against, that's clear.

The vast majority of the people today support Fidel, socialism, and what Fidel and socialism represent: sovereignty, education, health care, social justice. There's no doubt about that.

Some of you were here the day of Che's funeral.[9] You saw how people lined the streets, in silence. It was truly exemplary. There was sincere homage to a person who gave his life for the ideals we are defending. It was an incredible thing, as was the ceremony in Santa Clara, which was very moving and impressive.

Our adversaries must know this. I believe the CIA knows it, the Pentagon knows it, and I also think Clinton knows it.

Raúl Castro and the FAR

BARNES: I'd like to ask you a question about Raúl. Raúl is a special target of propaganda in the United States. With Fidel, the U.S. rulers tried especially hard to assassinate him; now they just hope as a mortal he goes away someday soon. As for Che, they hope to sell some Che T-shirts, beer, and watches, and they pray that young people don't get too interested po-

---

received more than 50 percent of the vote, a second round took place October 26. Municipal elections are held every two and a half years.

9 See interview with López Cuba, page 36, and interview with Villegas, pages 160–61.

litically. But they are always going after Raúl. He is bad, maybe even worse than Fidel.

I've always been very struck by this. I was in Cuba in the summer of 1960 for several months, and I learned firsthand the leadership standing Raúl had earned in the Rebel Army and during the first year and half of the new revolutionary government and Revolutionary Armed Forces. I think the U.S. rulers fear that continuity of the Cuban revolution. They fear the integrity of the army and its closeness to the Cuban people.

During the trial of General Ochoa and the others a number of years ago, I remember seeing some television footage from Cuba of the Military Court of Honor and of the review of the sentences by the Council of State. One look at Raúl's face revealed the pain he felt because of what had happened in the Revolutionary Armed Forces, even if it was an isolated thing. Soon afterwards Furry [Gen. Abelardo Colomé Ibarra] was named to head the Ministry of the Interior, and it seemed to us that the army was taking even more responsibility for the honor and the direction of the Cuban revolution.

So we would like to get out a little more of the truth about Raúl, whose place in the revolution is hidden from many, above all in the United States. And perhaps you could tell us how you view the responsibility of the armed forces in the march forward of the revolution, the honor and integrity of the FAR, and its internationalism.

FERNÁNDEZ: Raúl is a revolutionary with great human qualities, very strong principles, and firmness in the cause we defend. He is a hard worker, organized, systematic, and disciplined. He is very demanding in his work—above all of himself, and then of others. If Fidel was the founder of the Rebel Army and the creator of its strategic conception, Raúl has been the one who implements. Through his hard work and capacities over more than thirty years, he has organized a solid Revolutionary Armed Forces, politically firm, trained, and capable of defending the country, and above all, prepared to do so side by side with the people, who are an integral part of it. The FAR is very closely tied to the people. What Camilo [Cienfuegos] said is true: the armed forces are the people in uniform.

Raúl is a man like any other. Forceful but extraordinarily affable, he has a very Cuban personality; he communicates very well with the people; loves children; is capable of telling stories, making jokes, and enjoying them. He'll chat with somebody, then go to another person's house, and then go do something else. Young people like Raúl very much. When he shows up at a youth event he sparks a true show of enthusiasm.

Raúl is very sincere in what he says, and he has a deep sensibility in dealing with others. He has many friends, and he knows how to be a friend, a father, a comrade, and a firm and demanding political and military leader. And he has the talent and ability for the positions he holds, and for any others he might take on.

I am sure, as you said, that Raúl was deeply shaken by the Ochoa affair, above all, as well as by what happened in the Ministry of Interior. This was something unexpected. Human beings can fail, and that's what happened with Ochoa. He lost his way, made a profound mistake, conducted himself incorrectly, and created a complex and difficult situation by his behavior.

In that period the enemy accused Raúl and other leaders of the revolution of drug trafficking. Ochoa's behavior—the contacts he and his emissaries had made, the acts they had carried out—compromised the integrity of the country's name.

Regardless of the prestige Ochoa may have had, he was never an outstanding leader of the army. He was a man with personal merits, known as a general who had played a certain role, but this did not alter the fact that measures had to be taken, and that they had to be strong ones, in accordance with the gravity of the deeds committed. As a member of the Council of State at the time, I took personal responsibility for those measures. I had to give an opinion, and I did so with conviction and without reservations.[10]

Cuba has been against drugs from day one. In fact, drugs are practically unknown among the people here. In the 1980s, when I was minister of education, I visited a Latin American country. When the minister of education of that country asked me what we were doing to fight drugs in the schools, I had to ask him twice: Which schools are you talking about? In primary and secondary school, he responded. I was appalled that an eleven- or twelve-year-old child could have access to drugs and be allowed to use them.

Bourgeois armies and revolutionary armies

WATERS: It would be useful to return to a point you made earlier about the difference between a bourgeois army and a revolutionary army—the difference in the treatment of soldiers, and the relations between soldiers and officers.

FERNÁNDEZ: As a rule, a bourgeois army imposes its command, with some variation, through law, through established norms based exclusively on hierarchy and rank. A socialist army, our army, also uses norms and requires obedience. But discipline is achieved through conscious methods, and the commanding officers derive their authority from the consent of their subordinates; they earn that authority every day by their ability, work, and example.

In this army nobody can give orders who is not respected, who does not have the approval of one's subordinates. Command, clearly, isn't conferred by elections, but it's essential to have the consent and approval of one's subordinates. The army requires very strict discipline; there can be no concessions on

---

10 On July 9, 1989, Cuba's Council of State reviewed the death sentences and all twenty-nine members, including Fernández, voted to ratify them. Fernández was minister of education at the time. The entire proceedings of the Council of State meeting, at which every single member spoke, were telecast throughout Cuba.

that. But it must be very just, very humane, and maintain the highest moral values.

There have been tremendous abuses in other armies we know, or have known. To me, the attitudes that exist in the U.S. Marine Corps and among its instructors are often bestial; they're often criminal, inhumane, and unworthy. They are truly contemptible in a military institution. I'm not talking about the young people who have drowned in the swamps. I'm talking about the dehumanizing and denigrating methods of treating young people. That is unacceptable. That is an example of the difference between the two types of armies.

When someone who exercises authority or enforces discipline must do so, this often rankles those who are the objects of the command. You have to remember, however, that in our armed forces there are the units of the party; there are units of the UJC [Union of Young Communists]. These organizations strive for discipline and at the same time defend and guarantee the rights of individuals. There are places where one may speak frankly and say everything, regardless of rank. That doesn't happen in other armies.

Battle in the Escambray

BARNES: You referred earlier to the fight against the bandits in the Escambray? Could we return to that?

During the conference that Mary-Alice and I took part in here, Compañero Balaguer[11] talked about the generation of leaders that won their spurs not in the struggle against Batista, but at Girón, and in fighting to clean the bandits out of the Escambray. But the Escambray is a chapter of the revolutionary struggle that is very little known in the United States today.

11 Cuban Communist Party leader José Ramón Balaguer gave the keynote address at an October 21–23, 1997, international conference on Socialism on the Threshold of the 21st Century, which Barnes and Waters had just participated in.

RIA DE CUBA

"Many cadres and leaders of the revolution received their fundamental political education in the *guerrilla* in the mountains." Néstor López Cuba

Top: Rebel Army volunteers at Ñico López School for Recruits, established by Che Guevara at Rebel Army camp in Las Villas, December 1958. **Bottom:** Fidel Castro (on mule) speaking to peasants in Sierra Maestra, early 1958.

COURTESY JOSÉ
RAMÓN FERNÁNDEZ
AND MUSEUM OF THE
REVOLUTION

"As the revolution itself dramatically unfolded it continually pushed us to become more conscious of the importance of building a new society." Harry Villegas

Top left: Funeral demonstration of 60,000 in Santiago de Cuba, July 31, 1957, for July 26 Movement leader Frank País, murdered by Batista army. **Middle left:** José Ramón Fernández during his 1956 court-martial for participating in unsuccessful revolt within the military against the dictatorship. **Bottom left:** Peasants in the Sierra Maestra being rounded up by troops of the tyranny. **This page:** Havana, January 1, 1959. Just-released prisoners, still in white prison clothes, arm themselves and form up, as Cuba's working people take over the streets and ensure the victory of the Rebel Army.

BOHEMIA

LEE LOCKWOOD

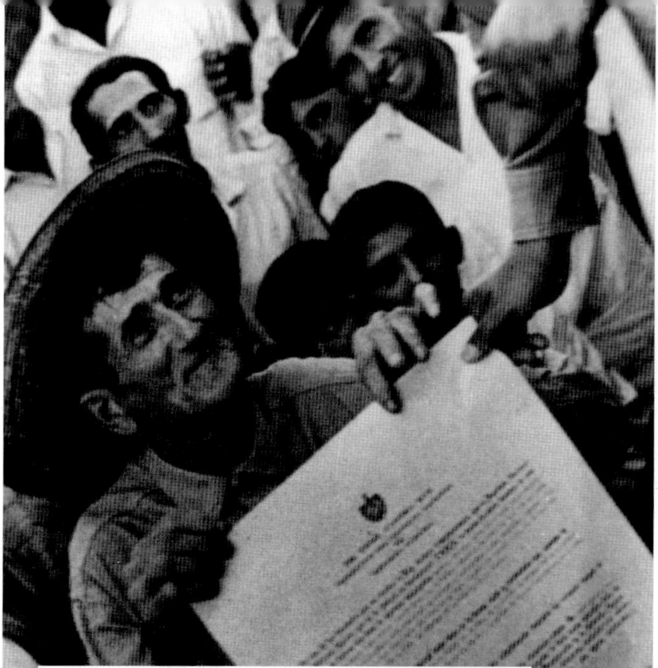

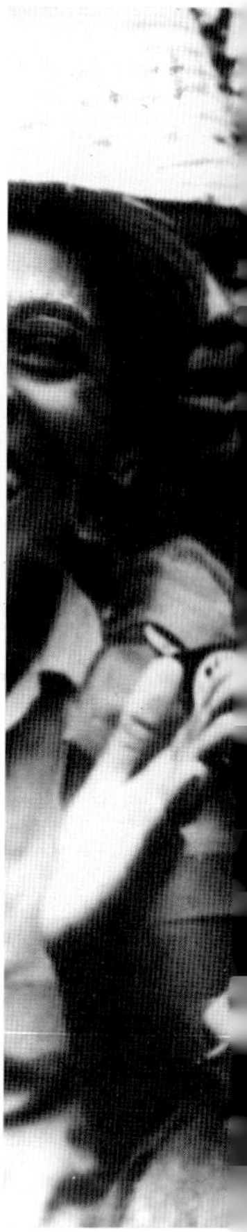

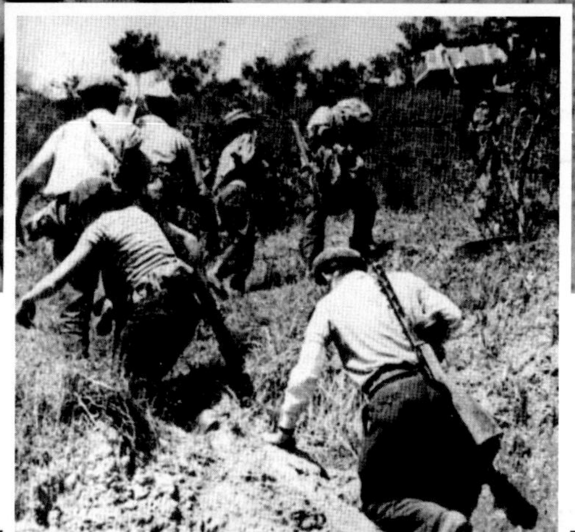

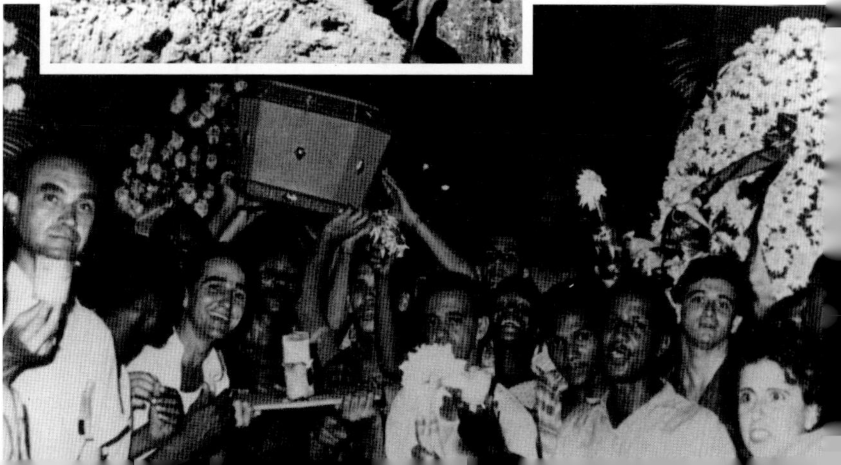

"The Rebel Army was the base of support for the gigantic task of transforming the political, economic, and social system." José Ramón Fernández

Top left: Peasant receives title to his land following Agrarian Reform Law in May 1959. **Middle left:** Members of the popular revolutionary militias pursuing counterrevolutionary bands in the Escambray, 1960 or 1961. **Bottom left:** Working people celebrate the expropriation of imperialist-owned interests in Cuba, August 1960. Marching through the streets of Havana, they are bearing coffins that symbolically contain the remains of enterprises such as Texaco and International Telephone and Telegraph, which were dumped in the sea. **This page top:** Literacy brigade volunteers returning to Havana in December 1961 to participate in mass rally at Ciudad Libertad, formerly the dictatorship's main military garrison in Havana. Completion of drive that taught hundreds of thousands to read and write effectively wiped out illiteracy in Cuba.

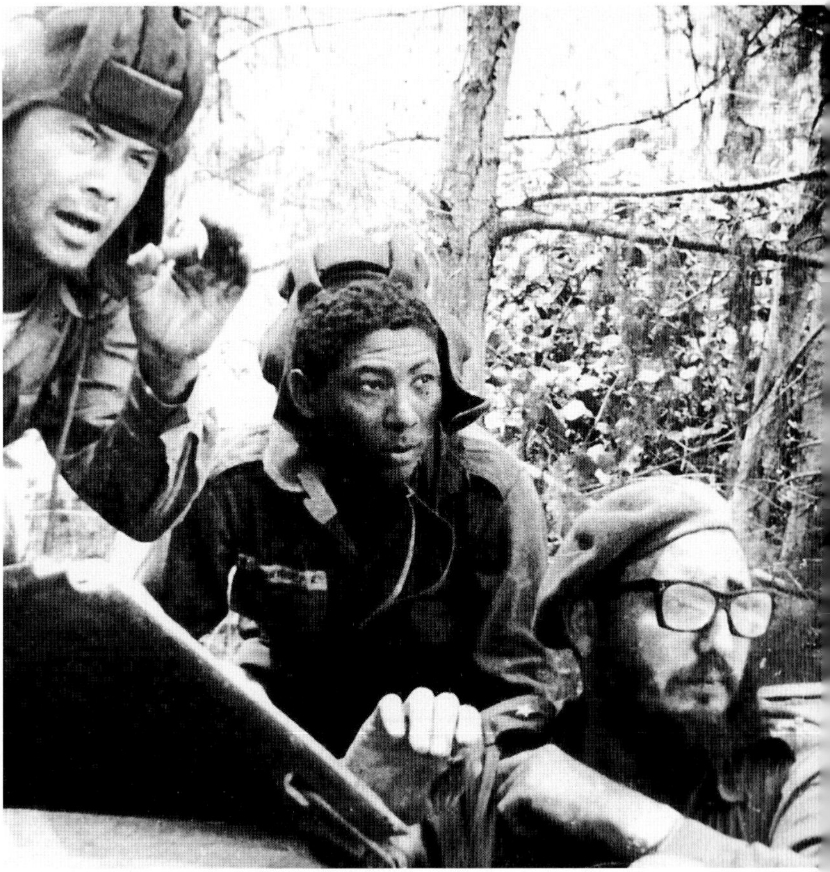

TOP LEFT AND FACING PAGE: GRANMA. FACING PAGE BOTTOM: JOSEPH HANSEN/MILITANT

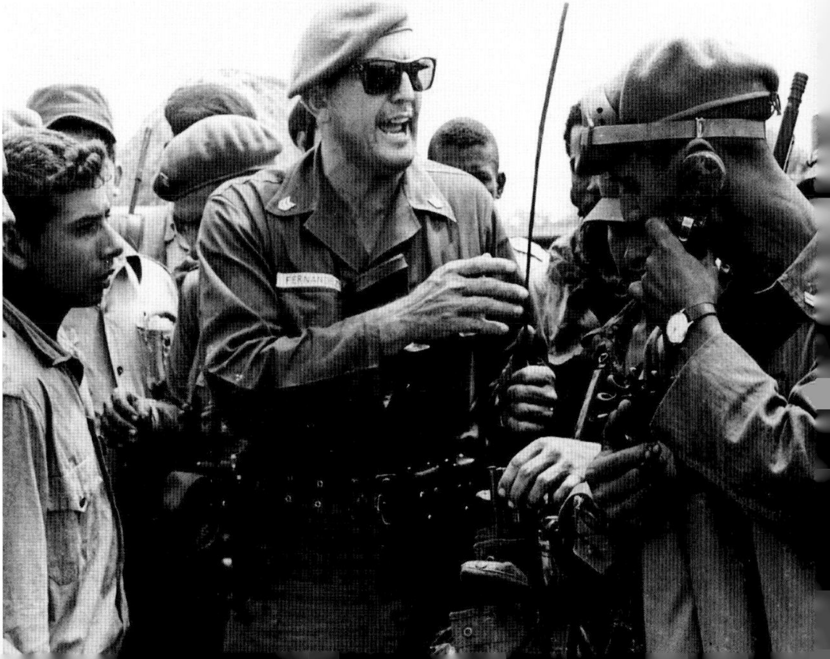

COURTESY JOSÉ RAMÓN FERNÁNDEZ

"You'd have to have lived through it to see how every Cuban, every worker, wanted to go to Girón." Harry Villegas

Top left: Fidel Castro with tank crew at Playa Girón. **Bottom left:** José Ramón Fernández, field commander of revolutionary forces, during the battle. **This page:** Cuban combatants on beach in front of wreckage of *Houston,* destroyed by Revolutionary Air Force. **Bottom right:** November 1960 picket line in front of United Nations in New York, called by Fair Play for Cuba Committee in support of the revolution.

FAIR PLAY FOR CUBA COMMITTEE

COURTESY ENRIQUE CARRERAS

"The stance of the Cuban people and its armed forces in defending Cuba during the October Crisis was decisive."
Néstor López Cuba

Top left: Néstor López Cuba in the Soviet Union, 1962, while attending military training school. **Bottom left:** Enrique Carreras, right, climbing into IL-28 transport plane, Pinar del Río, Cuba, during October 1962 crisis. **Top right:** Cuban militia members during the October crisis. Signs read, "No more tolerance for things poorly done" and "We stand firm, together with Fidel." **Bottom right:** United States U-2 spy plane shot down over Cuba by missile fired by Soviet antiaircraft unit, October 1962.

PHOTOS THIS PAGE: GRANMA

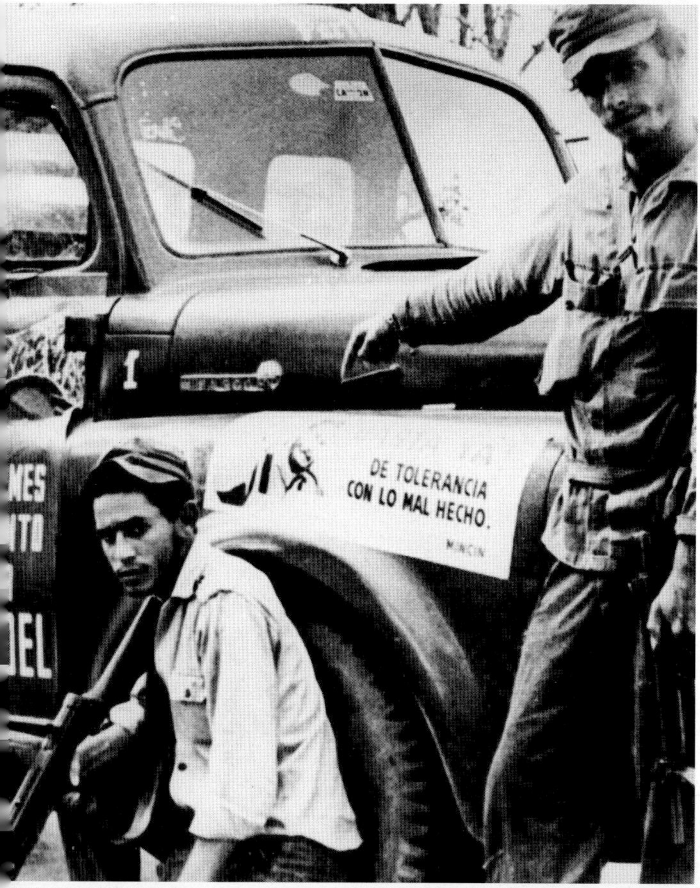
DE TOLERANCIA
CON LO MAL HECHO.

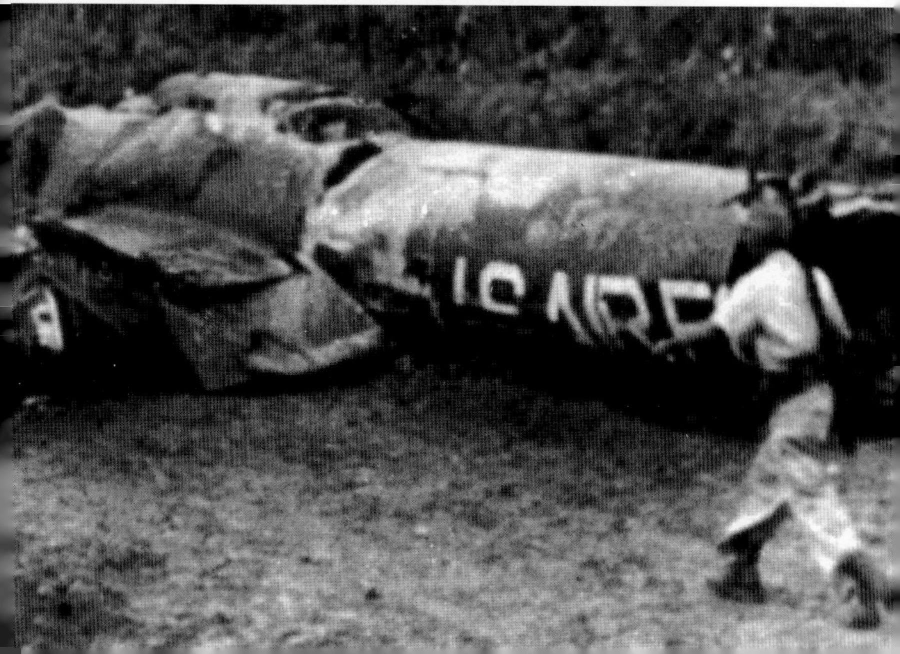

COURTESY ENRIQUE CARRERAS

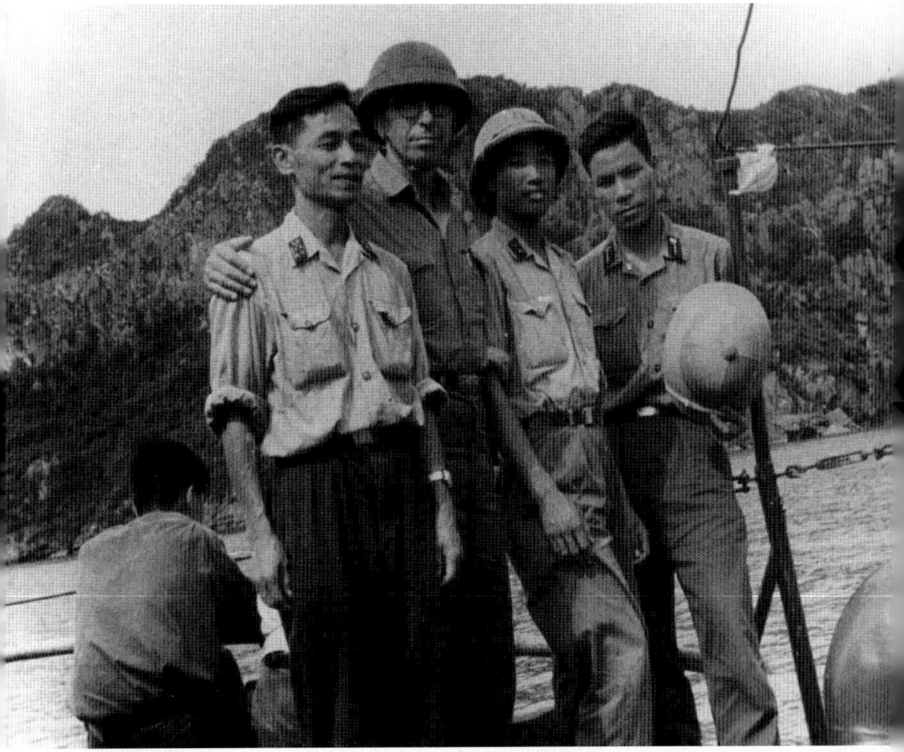

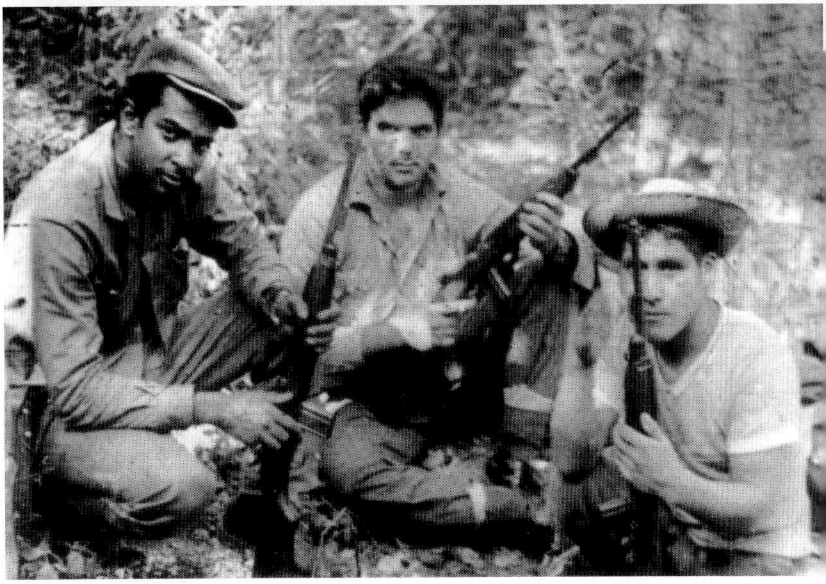

TRICONTINENTAL

"Our internationalist missions have been a catalyst
for the values that exist among the Cuban people."
Néstor López Cuba

Top left: Enrique Carreras, second from left, in Halong Bay, North Vietnam,
July 1969, as part of delegation studying Vietnamese antiaircraft defense tactics.
Bottom left: Harry Villegas (Pombo), left, together with Cuban and Bolivian
guerrilla fighters Pacho and Serapio in Bolivia, late 1966. **Top right:** Néstor
López Cuba (center) with other Cuban combatants in Nicaragua, 1988.
Bottom right: Cuban fighters in the Congo, 1965. Left to right: Roberto
Chaveco, Rogelio Oliva, José María Martínez Tamayo (Mbili, Papi), Che Guevara.

"The war of the entire people is the foundation of our tactics and strategy." Enrique Carreras

Top left: Cuban working people receive regular military training during monthly Defense Day exercise. **Bottom left:** Raúl Castro, minister of the Revolutionary Armed Forces. **Top right:** A woman's company of the Territorial Troop Militia in Havana during Defense Day target practice. **Bottom right:** Cuban soldiers visiting art museum.

GRANMA

FUERZAS ARMADAS REVOLUCIONARIAS

"The armed forces has set an example. It has shown that *sí se puede* — 'Yes, we can do it.'"
José Ramón Fernández

Top right: Rally of 70,000 people support Cuban revolution at University of Havana on September 7, 1994. Banner quoting Cuban national hero José Martí reads "Revolution: 'All I have done til today and all I will do tomorrow is for that.'" **Bottom left:** Members of volunteer minibrigade constructing housing in Havana, 1990. The minibrigades were a centerpiece of the rectification process of the late 1980s. **Bottom middle:** Contingent of volunteer workers composed of UJC members and other youth packing bananas in Holguín province, September 1994. Measures to increase food production were vital to meet challenge of Special Period in 1990s. **Bottom right:** Santa Clara, October 1997. Remains of Che Guevara and other revolutionists who fell in Bolivia are welcomed back to Cuba as a "reinforcement detachment."

OLUCION

"...hasta hoy, y haré, es para eso" *Hasta Ché*

LAURA GARZA/MILITANT

MARTÍN KOPPEL/MILITANT

PHOTOS: TOP, ARGIRIS MALAPANIS/MILITANT, BOTTOM, LINDA JOYCE/MILITANT

"They are afraid of Cuba. They are afraid
the example of our revolution could spread."
Enrique Carreras

Top: Brig. Gen. Harry Villegas talking with young people at World Youth
Festival in Havana, August 1997. **Bottom:** Cuban youth leaders Luis
Ernesto Morejón (third from left) and Itamys García Villar (in line, sixth from
left) talking with U.S. farmers in southern Georgia, March 1999.

It's important for revolutionaries in the United States to learn about this. Many of us spent time in Nicaragua, and we closely followed the Nicaraguan revolution. We watched with concern as we saw methods being used there to defeat the U.S.-organized counterrevolutionary forces evolve in a manner that finally compromised the Sandinistas' ability to win the political battle in the countryside. For that reason, among others, the question of the Escambray is very important for workers and youth who try to draw lessons from the Cuban revolution.

FERNÁNDEZ: I only participated in the Escambray on two occasions. Each time it was for one week, commanding some special unit that had been called up to fight there. But the battalions under my command that were training in Havana, at least those from the militias, were the principal forces in the mission to eliminate the bands in the Escambray.

The fight in the Escambray was conducted mainly by the militia units. The Escambray was an artificial situation created by U.S. agencies in late 1960 and early 1961 to promote subversion in Cuba. One of its aims was to provoke general uprisings and convert them into a force that would coincide in time and place and would cooperate with the invading brigade that landed at Playa Girón, which was initially scheduled to land at Trinidad.

Pardon me for a second. [*Fernández goes to get a map.*]

This is a tourist map of Cuba—the country is 1,200 kilometers [740 miles] from east to west, 100 kilometers [60 miles] from north to south, on average. Here is Trinidad, where the Girón landing was originally going to be. Kennedy was against it, since it's next to a city and was going to be too much of a scandal. That's part of history; it's in all the books.

Instead, the landing took place here, [*pointing to the map*] at Playa Girón in the Bay of Pigs. And the Escambray [*pointing*] is here. In other words, promoting counterrevolutionary groups in the Escambray was part of the preparation for the invasion and was timed to coincide precisely with the landing. The Escambray was to serve as a base of support, creating a zone that could be dominated by the invading brigade and by enemy forces in general. The invasion force left from here [*pointing to the map*]—from Nicaragua. They had trained in Guatemala. Then they moved over to Puerto Cabezas on Nicaragua's Atlantic Coast, and from there they were originally going to come to this place, to Trinidad.

The CIA created those groups with the support of Cuban agents. The Florida station of the CIA was at that time the largest in the world—that's a fact recorded in the CIA's own books, not in our imagination. Many Cubans who had abandoned the country joined the mercenary force: many former officers of the old army; sons of landowners, of rich people; extended families of the bourgeoisie; and also a fair number of lumpen. They were paid as soldiers, at wages that were high for the time. They were recruited in Miami and sent to Guatemala, where they formed a brigade.

The command of all the battalions in the invading brigade, and all the company commanders, were former officers of the old army. When we took them prisoner, I knew all the commanding officers by name. A good number of them had been my students before the revolution, when I was an instructor and assistant director of the school for cadets.

During the time there were bandits in the Escambray, planes flew over Cuba daily. There's a book called *Operation Puma*, in which a former air force captain of the old army explains how many flights he made on behalf of the CIA, dropping food, weapons, medicine, and communications equipment for the bandits in the Escambray. Those bands had no popular support, although it would be fair to say that some landowners from the area did back them. In many cases the support they received was obtained through coercion and terror.

The Rebel Army and the militia never killed a prisoner, tortured a prisoner, nor abandoned a single wounded enemy soldier—not during the struggle in the Sierra, not in the struggle against the bandits, not at Girón. That is a matter of principle, of ethics, in our armed forces, one Fidel has strictly demanded from the beginning of the revolutionary struggle. And this was important during the struggle against Batista. There were soldiers who were taken prisoner two or three times. They would be taken prisoner, disarmed, turned over to the Red Cross, and a few months later they would be taken prisoner again. This demoralized Batista's army, because contrary to Batista's propaganda, which said the Rebel Army killed prisoners, whenever soldiers were in danger they preferred to put up their hands and turn over their weapons. And that earned the Rebel Army great authority.

In December 1960 and January 1961 there was a great mobilization in Havana.[12] Some 40,000 men mobilized into forty battalions of almost a thousand each. A cordon, a physical barrier, was formed around the entire Escambray. Some militia members participated in that cordon for a month and a half, two months—militiamen with their weapons ready, protected from inclement weather only by nylon tarps, stayed firm, to prevent anyone from entering or leaving. The bands were practically eliminated. Thus, when the attack at Girón came, the invaders got no support either there or in the cities. Because in the cities, the Ministry of the Interior, the police, and the militias and the people were providing information: "So-and-so is not a revolutionary and is conspiring; he is meeting with others and they are conspiring against the revolution. Hold so-and-so in preventive detention." Whenever there were signs of counterrevolutionary activity, the persons would be detained, taken to the indoor sports complex, and watched, in the best possible conditions.

As a result, during the battle at Girón, in our rear guard, there was not a single enemy action. There was nothing, everything was calm. And that allowed us to conduct actions secure in our rear guard, and with great confidence.

When the battle was over at Girón, and people started being

12 See cover photo.

released from preventive detention, it turned out that—among the detainees—we had captured several CIA networks. That is, among those held in preventive detention for three days were persons who were counterrevolutionaries but were released since there was no proof they had done anything. There were others, however, against whom there was proof of crimes committed, and they were brought before the tribunals.

In the Escambray today there is no trace of any trauma. No peasant can say his child was killed by the revolutionary forces, or that he was tortured for protecting a band of insurgents. Some of those insurgents knew people or had family in the Escambray.

Many resources were used to eliminate these bands armed by the CIA. There was a famous group that wanted to head off to the United States. A film about them was made here. A small boat was outfitted, flying the U.S. flag, with people aboard who spoke English. It approached the northern coast and flashed false messages to this group, and the leader boarded with his band. But it was actually a Cuban boat, stocked with U.S. cigars, soft drinks, whisky. Members of the band were told to go below to get their shots, since they had to be vaccinated to enter U.S. territory. When they went down the stairs, there were two members of the Rebel Army below who seized their weapons and took them prisoner. There are numerous anecdotes like this.

Bought and paid for by Washington

These gangs of bandits were always fed, paid, supplied, and inspired by the United States, by its agencies of espionage and subversion.

They focused on the Escambray, but there were counterrevolutionary gangs throughout the country—we estimate there were more than five thousand bandits, in small bands in various places. It was the Cuban people who wiped them out; the militias were the ones who mainly fought against these bands.

After the bandits had been defeated in the Escambray, we

carried out a combination of political work and efforts to sat-
isfy, to the best of our ability, the peasants' material needs.
Today more than 95 percent of the housing units in Cuba have
electricity—even though they may be isolated houses. The
poverty-stricken thatch-roof, dirt-floor huts from before the
revolution have disappeared. There are roads and telephones
in many places. Peasants have schools, doctors, food supplies,
and agricultural assistance.

There are 150,000 small farmers who have title to their land
in Cuba. Their land rights have been and continue to be respected. We have taken many measures in the countryside. In
1994 and 1995 three million hectares [almost 7.5 million acres]
of land—nearly half the land in cultivation in Cuba—were
turned over to the Basic Units of Cooperative Production
(UBPCs) that grow sugarcane, raise cattle, and cultivate fruit,
along with growing many other crops.

We did not fight the counterrevolutionary bandits using
criminal methods. Assistance was given to their families. If
someone who died—including those who had betrayed the
Rebel Army—had children in an isolated rural area, those children were offered scholarships. In other words, our revolution has had a deeply humane spirit, which in turn has increased its prestige.

We are sometimes accused of violating human rights. As
our foreign minister has pointed out, this is part of a selective
campaign carried out by our adversaries to create hostility
against Cuba and undermine our prestige. As far as I am concerned, the first human right is the right to live, to receive an
education, to live with dignity, to have the possibility of always receiving health care, to a job, to hold a place in society
based on one's capacities, technical training, talent, and de-
sires. And to have a right to a country that exists with dignity,
as a sovereign nation.

Not a single prisoner has been tortured here in Cuba; not a
single person has disappeared—not one, in thirty-eight years.
Who among those who accuse us of human rights violations,

or who act as accomplices by voting to condemn us, could raise their hand and say the same thing? We do not permit anyone to be mistreated for reasons of sex, religion, or the color of one's skin. I'd like to know how the human rights of Hispanic immigrants or Blacks are observed in the United States. Look at California, Florida, New York. Could they say what I have just said? They can exert pressure and muster votes to condemn us, but they are following a selective policy toward us, and we do not feel guilty.

Few places guarantee human rights as Cuba does—not just in word but in deed. Very few—if anyone—among those who condemn us on the basis of human rights has any moral standing whatsoever to do so. That's a point I wanted to be sure to make, since we have spoken of struggle, of ethics, and of morality.

We are poor, but we have dignity. We are not ashamed of our poverty. We would be ashamed to be rich as a result of theft, of exploitation, of corruption. We would be ashamed to become rich that way.

The Special Period and rectification

BARNES: We'd like to ask you one question about the Special Period. We've followed developments in Cuba in recent years closely and written about them. One thing we've noticed is that workers and youth in the United States who look to the revolution often seem to draw a sharp divide between the Special Period of the 1990s and the rectification process that began in the latter half of the 1980s. We've tried to explain that this is not accurate—that the political rearming of the revolution that was at the heart of rectification, the place of Che and the reconquering of a truly communist course, are all deeply connected with the capacity of the Cuban people and youth to understand and meet the challenges of the Special Period.

We shouldn't look at the efforts to overcome the crisis of the Special Period as just an economic matter, we've explained. Che never looked at anything that way. He always pointed to the connections between economics and politics that were central to advancing the march toward socialism.

The Revolutionary Armed Forces has a key role in the struggle to confront the Special Period. The army not only guarantees every Cuban a rifle, a grenade, and a land mine to defend the revolution, but has also set an example in production and discipline. As you remarked in answering a previous question, the army is very close to the people.

No one who has been here in Cuba for the last three weeks during the party congress and the solemn ceremony in Santa Clara you described earlier—as Martín and Mary-Alice have been for most of that period, and as I've been for the past week—could fail to recognize the popular affirmation of the communist course of Fidel and Che registered in these events. No one could confuse Cuba with what was presented as socialism for so long in the Soviet Union and Eastern Europe. No one could fail to see the deep connection between moving forward in the Special Period and preparing new generations in Cuba for their revolutionary internationalist role in the world that is coming.

So, we would like to hear any of your views that would help us better understand the challenges of the Special Period, the place of the army in it, and its connection to the political course that Che and Fidel fought for and exemplify.

FERNÁNDEZ: If you look at the newspapers in Cuba dated April 20, 1986, you'll find Fidel's speech from the day before, entitled "The Rectification of Errors and Negative Tendencies." It was given at the main rally on the anniversary of Playa Girón, April 19, 1986.

No one at that time was thinking about the fall of socialism—the collapse not of the ideas of socialism, but of the methods used in the work, in the goals of the parties claiming to be constructing socialism. For me, socialism remains the same today as it was in the 1980s—a just idea, one that seeks to create a society that will eliminate inequalities and make human beings the central element, the reason for its existence.

But we had copied certain things, believing that those who had seventy years of experience were doing them well.

For a number of years, however, we had begun to see things that did not really lead to the objectives we were pursuing. Fidel had understood that the policies being followed here in Cuba not only on the economic level but in many other areas were deeply flawed. We had copied and imitated, and were carrying out many things we should not have been doing.

Our party has always been very much linked to the masses. In Cuba, for someone to be taken into the Communist Party, that person has to be approved by the collective decision of both members and nonmembers at their workplace. It is a highly selective process, based on the qualities, merits, and prestige of the individual.

I am speaking of 1986. The collapse of the socialist camp did not begin to become visible until 1988 or 1989. It is natural to think that everything took place within the framework of a single conception of perfecting things. But clearly the Special Period gave rise to very concrete conditions that implied there had to be modifications in some of the actions we had taken within the rectification process.

We lost 85 percent of our trade overnight. We used to get 14 million tons of fuel, a figure that was reduced to zero. We used to get spare parts, transportation equipment, machinery for our factories, cereals, and other food products. We used to export sugar, nickel, and other products at mutually advantageous prices—at what I would call just prices. If the price of machinery or chemical products went up, so too would the price of the products or raw materials we were exporting over there. A just exchange between rich and poor.

This is a world in which the rich countries, the rich societies, tend to become richer, despite the fact that there are also poor people there. And the poor societies are becoming poorer and poorer. This is what is happening in Africa, and to a large degree in Latin America.

So we took measures. I remember when the minister of the

armed forces [Raúl Castro] invited the central leaders of the government to a meeting of criticism and self-criticism, pointing concretely to what we needed to rectify and modify.

The FAR was the first to make these rectifications. With Raúl's leadership capacity, his capacity as a statesman, and his energy and firmness in putting forward ideas, he carried out genuine transformations in the FAR. The FAR today is largely self-sufficient, with the exception of sugar and salt, producing 80 to 90 percent of everything it consumes. It cultivates land and raises livestock. And the FAR pays for what it buys—it doesn't simply have land that it tills with fertilizer, fuel, and fodder it is given. It implements rigorous methods and economic controls.

The FAR has shown in practice the levels of efficiency that can be attained. The Youth Army of Labor, made up of young people called up for service, has shown that it is a highly productive and efficient force.

In other words, the army, the armed forces, sets an example. When I use the word "army," it is because the Rebel Army was the soul, the seed, the nucleus around which all the various armed institutions were created in Cuba. It has shown that *sí se puede*—"We can do it"—as Raúl says. There are some people, when faced with difficulties—those without initiative—who say, "No, it cannot be done." Raúl has shown that, "Yes, it can be done." And he began preaching this by example.

That's the way things are with the armed forces. The armed forces continue to provide training, maintaining their capacity for combat—I would say they have increased it. At the same time, they are producing, feeding themselves, and in some cases providing something additional for the state.

I, of course, don't see the Special Period as a consequence of rectification. But I do see it as linked to rectification, in the effort to find the methods, to find the correct course to follow, to find solutions that the country needs to emerge victorious.

'We are a political army, fully aware of what we are defending'

BRIGADIER GENERAL HARRY VILLEGAS

Top: Brig. Gen.
Harry Villegas
during interview.

Bottom: Villegas
(at right) in Angola,
1980s.

Harry Villegas

BRIG. GEN. HARRY VILLEGAS was born in 1940 in Yara, a small village in the foothills of the Sierra Maestra mountains of eastern Cuba. As a teenager he joined the struggle against the U.S.-backed dictatorship of Fulgencio Batista and in 1957 became a member of the Rebel Army, fighting under the command of Ernesto Che Guevara. Villegas served in Guevara's command-post platoon and in the fall of 1958 was part of the Rebel Army's invasion of Las Villas province in central Cuba. In December 1958 he took part in the battle of Santa Clara. The capture of Cuba's third-largest city on January 1, 1959, by the Rebel Army sealed the fate of the Batista regime.

After the victory of the revolution in January 1959, Villegas served as head of Guevara's personal escort. In 1961, following Cuba's nationalization of imperialist- and domestically owned industry, he worked with Guevara as a factory administrator in the broadening effort to lead Cuban working people to take more direct control of the organization of the economy. He returned to active military duty the following year.

In 1965 Villegas volunteered for an internationalist mission in the Congo, where he was chief adjutant to Guevara, who led the front. It was during this campaign that Villegas received the nom de guerre he has used ever since: Pombo.

He is best known around the world as one of the Cuban revolutionaries who fought alongside Guevara in Bolivia in 1966–67 in a campaign to establish a revolutionary front in Latin America's Southern Cone. He served on the general staff

throughout the eleven-month Bolivian campaign. After Guevara was killed in October 1967, Villegas commanded the group
of surviving combatants that eluded the encirclement jointly
organized by the Bolivian army and U.S. military forces and
the CIA. Following numerous battles, three surviving Cuban
combatants crossed the border into Chile in February 1968
and arrived in Cuba the following month.

Villegas's account of the 1966–68 revolutionary campaign in
Bolivia is published under the title *Pombo: A Man of Che's 'guerrilla.'*

Between 1975 and 1990, Villegas was part of the leadership
of the Cuban volunteer military contingent in Angola. He
served as front commander and a member of the general staff;
member of the general staff of Operation Olive (the struggle
against right-wing bands); liaison between the military mission and the armed forces command in Havana; and head of
operations. In 1995 the Council of State awarded Villegas the
status of Hero of the Republic of Cuba, the country's highest
honor.

In recent years he was head of the Political Section of Cuba's
Western Army, and a member of the Political Directorate of
the General Staff of the Revolutionary Armed Forces (FAR).
Currently he heads the Secretariat and is ideological director
of the Patriotic-Military and Internationalist Front of the Association of Combatants of the Cuban Revolution. He is also a
deputy to the National Assembly of People's Power and a
member of the Central Committee of the Communist Party of
Cuba.

The interview with Harry Villegas was conducted in Havana on November 10, 1998, by Mary-Alice Waters and Martín
Koppel.

'We are a political army, fully aware of what we are defending'

MARY-ALICE WATERS: The region of eastern Cuba where you were born and raised has throughout history been the cradle of revolutionary struggle in Cuba, the stronghold of the independence forces for more than a century and a half. How did these traditions affect you as a youth? What experiences led you to join the revolutionary struggle to overthrow the Batista dictatorship?

HARRY VILLEGAS: Oriente has been the birthplace of all of Cuba's independence struggles. In fact, this was even where the first rebel in Cuba, and the first Cuban internationalist, you might say—the Indian Hatuey—started fighting. Hatuey was a native of the island of Quisqueya—or Española, which was the name given it by the colonizers; today it is the Dominican Republic.

Oriente's revolutionary traditions

I think there are two major reasons why the people from Oriente have been a decisive force from the beginning in our struggles for independence, both of which are closely interrelated. One is economic. Oriente was one of the poorest areas, with the highest illiteracy rate, cut off from social development. Here in Cuba we say that struggles come from the east—that independence came from the east—but culture comes from the west. The revolution has evened this out somewhat, making things more equitable. But Oriente was really much more backward than the western provinces. The other factor was that exploitation by the powers that be, and the repression, were more intense there. This generated dissatisfaction and protests. It generated acts of violence.

If you go back to 1868, to the first independence war, the people from Oriente were the ones who adopted the most radical positions. Their starting point was always the need for independence. There were other tendencies, such as the annexationists and the reformists, but the people from Oriente always fought hardest for independence.[1]

Over time traditions developed. The war of 1868, led by Carlos Manuel de Céspedes, began in Oriente. The war of 1895 spread a little more to other parts of the country—there were uprisings in Havana, Matanzas, Las Villas, and elsewhere. But the deepest uprisings were in Oriente—not only in Baire,[2] but also in Guantánamo and several other places in the province.

The traditions of struggle in this region continued, passed along through families and schools. Jesús Menéndez, the "General of the Canefields," was murdered in cold blood in Oriente in 1948. He was from Santa Clara, not Oriente, although he had support there. And they killed him while he was visiting the sugar mills.

In 1952, following Batista's coup d'état, resistance in Oriente was boiling. People hoped somebody would step forward to lead the fight. Then came the attack on Moncada in 1953, the *Granma* landing in 1956. The struggle exploded everywhere. Oriente was on a war footing.

By then, Celia Sánchez's influence had been greatly felt in the

1 There were two important Cuban wars of independence from Spain: the war of 1868–78, and the war of 1895–98 that ended in Spain's defeat. Cuba became an independent republic, but its government was in fact dominated by U.S. occupation forces. See glossary notes, Annexationists.

2 Cuba's final war of independence began in 1895 in a series of uprisings, including one in Baire that became known as *El Grito de Baire* (the Cry of Baire).

area where I lived. And the July 26 Movement—Celia, that is—had won over a number of peasants to support the *Granma* landing. In Manzanillo and surrounding urban areas, there was some organization in the underground struggle, fostered by Celia. The incorporation of the first peasants in the Sierra Maestra didn't come about spontaneously. Celia had made contact with Guillermo García, with Crescencio Pérez, with Ciro Frías. In other words, she had organized a whole group of peasants who quickly stepped in to support the *Granma* expeditionaries.

I had a brother who belonged to a cell of the July 26 Movement. So when the tyranny reacted to the revolutionary struggle by intensified repression, we really felt it firsthand.

The upsurge in revolutionary struggle in response to these epic events, these legendary battles, had a profound impact on the young people of the region. That's why there were very few young men in the vicinity of the Sierra Maestra who did not go up to the mountains to join the Rebel Army. That's why there were so many combatants from Yara and Bayamo and Manzanillo. This direct influence led people to join the revolutionary struggle.

My participation began in an underground cell, carrying out small actions like throwing chains over electrical wires in order to cut power, planting small bombs, distributing propaganda, selling bonds to raise money. In a small town, the normal things one does become known very quickly, and the authorities singled us out, trying to stop these actions. They arrested me two or three times and slapped me around. A cousin of mine and my mother stepped in. They would automatically go down to the garrison to see what was happening. Because you know how these small towns are. Yara was a tinderbox. Word spread rapidly. "So-and-so is in jail," they would say. Right away the entire family headed over to the garrison.

It was getting harder and harder to live there. It was a very small town, very tiny. And the army maintained a permanent presence in the vicinity. It became an important center for the army, with battalions of troops stationed there. There were

more soldiers in Yara than residents. You couldn't go anywhere without running into a soldier.

At one point, early in the struggle, the general staff of the
tyranny's army was in the Estrada Palma sugar mill, now called
Bartolomé Masó. It's right next to Yara, in the same foothills.
To get to Estrada Palma, you had to pass through Yara.

So we asked for authorization from the movement to go up
to the Sierra. They didn't give it to us, but since we were a
little undisciplined, we went and joined up anyway.

WATERS: Earlier today you mentioned informally a fact I
found very striking, that six generals currently in the Revolutionary Armed Forces come from Yara.

VILLEGAS: Among the many fighters that Yara produced,
and it produced a lot of them, six have attained the rank of
general.

WATERS: Did you all know each other back then?

VILLEGAS: It's a very small town, so it would be pretty hard
not to have known each other.[3] Division General Leopoldo
Cintra Frías, a Hero of the Republic of Cuba, came from that
town. You also have the first and only woman to have earned
the rank of general in Cuba, Teté Puebla—Delsa Puebla, but
we call her Teté. Then there's Manuel Lastre, brigadier general; Miguel Lorente, also a brigadier general. And there's
Orestes Guerra. Plus myself. There are six of us. The town of
Yara really did produce a lot of fighters for the Rebel Army.

Fight against racist discrimination

WATERS: What differences were there between blacks and
whites? Was the struggle against racial oppression part of your
rebellion against the existing social, economic, and political
conditions?

VILLEGAS: Discrimination in this region was not very severe. Its effects were not greatly felt. I don't know the rea-

3 In the late 1950s Yara had a civilian population of seven- to ten thousand.

sons why. It might be because we had a little money. I come from a poor family, but my mother had a store and we were slightly better off.

But Oriente wasn't like Las Villas, for example. If you went to a park in Las Villas—just to point out the kind of discrimination there—blacks walked through one part of the park and whites through another. This was not the case in Yara. There blacks and whites walked together, and blacks and whites mixed at fiestas.

There were separate social clubs, of course. White and black were separate. Blacks could not go to parties and dances at white clubs. But they played sports together. They went to the same schools. In other words, discrimination there wasn't as severe as in other parts of the country.

Perhaps it was because my region was more isolated. Perhaps because Yara was very close to where slaves were first freed in Cuba, right there in La Demajagua. Or perhaps because the first slaves who fought for Cuba's independence were those from Yara, on October 11, 1868.[4] These things too may have had an influence.

My grandfather was a sergeant in the *mambí* army. He fought in Maceo's invasion column. He was one of those who fought for independence in the region around Yara. So he was very respected in town. He was regarded with a great deal of affection. Perhaps these were all reasons why we didn't suffer much discrimination, why we didn't experience its full effects.

After the triumph of the revolution, however, I had a chance to see what discrimination really was. I remember returning to Havana en route from Yara. It was the first time after the victory of the revolution I'd gone home. They had given me a pass, and I had gone to see my family. I was nineteen years old at the time. We stopped at one town in Las Villas, the last one you come to on the Central Highway going west before getting to Matanzas; I think it's called Los Arabos. A dance

4 See glossary notes, Yara, Grito de.

was going on and we went in. I was with Alberto Castellanos, who is white. Both of us were in Che's personal escort, and we went around together.

When we walked into the hall, we saw everybody going "shhhhh," making comments to each other. I really didn't notice at first. They sent for a police officer who was black to come tell us we couldn't be there because that club was for whites only. "Who says this is for whites only?" we replied. "And why did you, a black man, agree to be sent here?" Castellanos added. We were wearing our officers' uniforms, and we started asking young women to dance with us, and they did. But then we thought, perhaps it wasn't such a good idea, nor was it the right thing, to go to this place they wanted to kick me out of.

Castellanos stepped in and said no, they couldn't kick me out. He couldn't accept that. If I had to leave, he would do so as well. We caused a stir. But in the end we had a huddle and decided to leave. Blacks were not expected to show up at their club.

The same thing happened to us here in Havana, in Tarará. After Che left La Cabaña, we moved to Tarará.[5] There was a club in Tarará that blacks were not permitted to enter. One day we went for a walk, and we went into the club. They sent for General Bayo to get us out. We respected Bayo; he was the general who served as instructor for the *Granma* expeditionaries in Mexico. And he told us we had to leave, because blacks could not be there. We asked how it was that he, who was so well respected and so well liked in the army, could fail to understand that we had not fought so blacks would continue being oppressed. But we left.

When I got home and told the story to the other members of the escort, however, they grabbed their rifles and went out

5 Tarará in prerevolutionary times was an area of luxury beachfront homes outside Havana. Diagnosed with exhaustion and pneumonia, Guevara was moved there for rest and recuperation at the beginning of March 1959 on doctor's orders, together with his family and escort. He remained there until May 1959.

and took over the club. They made everyone leave saying, "This is now the Rebel Army's club." Later Bayo went and told Che about it. Che then spoke to us, telling us we shouldn't do things like that, because they could be utilized by the enemy. He said the revolution had not yet progressed far enough for people to understand that there were neither blacks nor whites, but rather that we are fighting for all Cubans, for equality, against discrimination.[6]

MARTÍN KOPPEL: What soldiers took over the club?

VILLEGAS: The soldiers under my command. I was head of Che's escort and I had a platoon there, at the beachfront in Tarará.

WATERS: On your orders?

VILLEGAS: No, they did it spontaneously. I didn't get involved. But these were more or less my experiences with discrimination. This was as close as I came to being directly affected by it.

Discrimination is always a rather complex phenomenon. It might not affect you directly, but you feel it. You could say it's a problem that lies in some people's subconscious, and they still have to be educated. I have known people who have told me, "I'll give my life for you, but I wouldn't let you marry my daughter because you're black."

Can you believe that?

WATERS: Yes, I can.

It seems that at that time in Oriente, blacks also owned land. That must have affected social relations as well.

VILLEGAS: There were regions of the country, like Las Villas, where discrimination was very severe. Blacks had their

6 On March 22, 1959, around the time of the events Villegas is describing, Cuban prime minister Fidel Castro gave a speech that came to be known as the revolutionary government's "Proclamation against Discrimination." In it he called for a campaign against unequal treatment of blacks in employment and public facilities. In the weeks following the speech, all whites-only facilities in Cuba were rapidly opened to everyone. Those refusing were closed down.

place as blacks. In Havana, too.

In Yara you didn't see really rich people. When I go to visit people now, for example, I realize I used to think so-and-so was rich, but now I realize he wasn't; he didn't have anything. He was a storekeeper just like us. With the same things, the same status, the same conditions of life. But he was white, and whites always had a little higher status. That's still the case in Cuba today. The revolution has created the conditions to end discrimination and is fighting to do so, but there are still those who will insult you to your face.

This also happens with women. We're fighting to end discrimination against women. But there are still people in the armed forces itself who think that women only cause us problems. When they have children, they take a maternity leave. The woman's job remains unoccupied for up to a year, and that causes conflicts. Of course, that doesn't mean we shouldn't have women in the armed forces; we've got many.

But they are not treated the same. We don't take disciplinary action against women. If a woman is absent, it's not the same as a man being absent. Women are not put on trial, but men are. It's a question of courtesy, and courtesy toward women is part of the revolutionary ethic.

The forging of a revolutionary

WATERS: As a young person you certainly didn't imagine that one day you would be a general in the Revolutionary Armed Forces. When you were growing up, what did you think you would do?

VILLEGAS: We Cubans don't like to be military men.

I never wanted to be in the military. I wanted to be a pilot. That was what I longed for, what most interested me. At home they wanted me to be a storekeeper like my mother, but that's not what I wanted.

My father was a worker, a carpenter. He had a shop where they made furniture and did construction work. He was in the army for a while when he was young. I never knew him when he was in the military, but my older brothers did. My father's family came from the Canary Islands, and he was a very educated man for our small town, uncommonly so. Very good at chess. He sat us down and taught us how to play. He used to play chess with all the kids in the neighborhood. My mother Engracia was of African descent. She had a shopkeeper's heart, and liked business, commerce. She started out making candy. Then she set up a little store in Yara Arriba, and later expanded it. After that she bought a little store in Las Tunas. Later on, she started a bakery with her sister in Palma.

My mother and father were two completely different types of people. My father was extremely kind. He had nothing. Everyone loved him. He was the best-loved person in town. Whenever he saw something that needed to be done, he did it. My mother put her family first, took care of her family, saw that the kids went to school. She was more self-centered, you might say. My father was a little more socialist, more open, kinder.

KOPPEL: How did your aspirations, your expectations, change with the revolutionary struggle?

VILLEGAS: When we went to the Sierra, pushed by the expanding struggle against the dictatorship, we didn't have a well-defined Marxist or Leninist political outlook. Simply a sense of justice. Our aim was to fight the system that existed, that was imposed on us, and to fight things that were wrong. Generally that's what motivated us and many others. Often people didn't even know why they went exactly. They simply got caught up in the spirit of the struggle and joined the people who were in the Sierra.

My brother had been a member of the Cuban People's (Orthodox) Party, the same party Fidel had belonged to. It embodied the most progressive section of Cuban youth at that time. Theoretically speaking, you might say, the most progressive elements should have been in the Popular Socialist Party. But from the point of view of the masses, the most progressive elements among Cuban youth at the time were in the Orthodox Party. And those young people in the Orthodox Party later joined the July 26 Movement under Fidel's leadership, my brother among them. As one might expect, he dragged me along with him toward those ideas. I was the youngest child, while he was the oldest.[7] And when my brother left town to join the Rebel Army, I stepped forward and threw myself into the work of the cell.

That was when my revolutionary activity began, without any theoretical foundation. Later, over time, reality itself took hold of my consciousness. When you arrived in the Sierra Maestra, you saw how the peasants lived, how they lacked everything, how they were truly exploited. When you spoke with them, they told you stories about how they had ended up in the Sierra Maestra, since they had no way to make a living, no way to support themselves, searching for a piece of land to provide for themselves by the sweat of their brow.

All these things had a radicalizing effect. When I met him, Che was concerned about the people's health. He would explain to us his ideas of justice and equality. How one had to work with the peasants to win them over, from an ideological point of view. How we had to engage in armed propaganda. How we weren't allowed to mistreat the peasants. These concepts would form part of the basis of our socialist ideas.

Later on, when the distribution of land began, Che explained to us why it was so urgent, why land distribution was a necessity. He was the first one to argue for agrarian reform. Che was the one who participated in drafting the first agrarian reform law in the Sierra,[8] and later he drafted one with Humberto Sorí Marín. Fidel was seeking a balance. A representative of the communist tendency and a representative of the

7 At the time Villegas was fourteen years old; his brother was thirty-five.
8 On October 19, 1958, the general command of the Rebel Army issued Law no. 3, on the peasants' right to the land. The law abolished tenant farming and sharecropping in liberated territories, and recognized all those who worked the land, including squatters, as the legitimate owners.

capitalist tendency. Sorí Marín was a lawyer, and Fidel paired him with Che in drafting the first agrarian reform law.

All these things had an influence on us. Later, the revolution itself, as it dramatically unfolded, continually pushed us to become more and more conscious of the importance of building a different society.

In my case, I was forced to read and study. I was very young and wanted to hang out and have a good time. But Che said, "Your first duty is to raise your educational level." He explained that we had to raise our educational level in order to be more useful to the revolution and to our people.

Then one day, he said to me, "You're a factory intervener."[9] I said, "Me?" "Yes, you. You're a factory intervener." Che sent me, with no training and little more than a sixth-grade education, to Sanitarios Nacionales, a factory just outside Havana (today it is in the municipality of San José) that produced bathroom fixtures and other ceramics. It was the first company we acquired that had been jointly held by foreign and domestic owners. It belonged to a Mexican and a Cuban. The revolution seized the assets that belonged to the Cuban, and left the part belonging to the Mexican alone. Those were the conditions under which I went there.

Playa Girón, October Crisis

WATERS: Several months ago we had the opportunity to interview three other generals of the Revolutionary Armed Forces about their experiences during Playa Girón and the October Crisis. We talked with Division Generals Néstor López Cuba and Enrique Carreras and Brigadier General José Ramón

9 After 1959, the new government took over the running of a number of economic enterprises held by Batista's cronies, as well as some public utilities. These actions, known as "interventions," were in turn directed by "interveners." Following Cuba's nationalization of foreign- and domestically owned capital between August and October 1960, the term came to be used to describe the revolutionary cadres assigned to head the workplaces in the newly nationalized industries.

Fernández. Each one had a unique perspective on those historic events, of course. And your experience during the days
of Playa Girón adds another element. You were working at
the ceramics factory you just mentioned and were not on active duty as an officer of the FAR. How did the working class
respond to the invasion?

This is important because Washington's hand was not stayed
primarily by Cuba's military strength, but by politics. They
feared the determination of Cuba's working people to defend
their revolution. They feared the price the U.S. armed forces
would have to pay. They didn't want to run the risk of invading Cuba, because the casualties would have been so high.

From your perspective at that time, working as intervener
at the ceramics factory, how did working people respond to
news of the invasion at Playa Girón?

VILLEGAS: At the time of the mercenary landing at Girón, I
had recently left Che's personal escort. In essence, I felt more
like a guard than a worker. So when they landed, I automatically reported to Che, ready to go there with him and participate in battle. Che had done the same thing.[10] He intended to
go fight. But everyone was ordered to stay at their assigned
post. Fidel told Che that he had to be at his assigned post in
Pinar del Río. The whole thing was totally organized. And
Che told me the same thing Fidel told him. "Stay in the factory," Che said. "You must remain at the helm, organizing the
defense, the security of the factory, and maintaining production."

Who responded when Cuba needed to be defended? Who
was called to service? The workers. Those who were mobilized in their volunteer militia battalions were sent off to Playa

10 At the time, Guevara was minister of industry. During the Playa Girón
   invasion, as well as the October Crisis of 1962, the revolution's central leaders were assigned command of troops in different regions of the country. On
   both occasions, Guevara was sent to head the defense of Pinar del Río,
   Cuba's westernmost province.

Girón. One of those who was killed there came from our factory, and it was subsequently named after him.

It's difficult to describe. You'd have to have lived through it to see how every Cuban, every worker, wanted to go to Girón. The workers wanted to leave the factory, and I had to stand there telling them that everyone had to carry out the task they were assigned to. Their task was to remain there and produce, because it was also important to maintain production. It was the same thing I had been told by Che. I had been convinced of it, and now in turn I had to convince others.

Nevertheless, many workers were pulled out. All those who were members of militia battalions and sub-battalions were sent to Girón. Everyone was anxious to know exactly what was happening. It was a challenge to maintain discipline, because every time the tanks went by, or the transport vehicles filled with men went by, everyone wanted to come out and watch, to cheer for them and wave, to see the militiamen off. My task was a very pedagogical one.

KOPPEL: And where were you in 1962 at the time of the October Crisis?

VILLEGAS: The October Crisis came when I was at the school for administrators. I was one of those who had become an administrator without ever even having been told what a factory was, so they told me I had to study. Che took me out of the factory and sent me to a school, a school for administrators, where there were about four hundred compañeros. While I was there at that school, the crisis hit.

Officers from the FAR general staff came there and explained to us that we were being formed into a unit of the reserves. They organized us and kept us on alert, waiting to see how things went. An officer came by frequently to brief us. But at first we didn't know exactly what was happening.

Soon we were given more complete information, about the blockade of the island ordered by the U.S. government. About our decision, the government's decision, which by that time had been made public, to not allow them to inspect us.[11] That would have been a humiliation, an affront to our dignity and our sovereignty. All those questions were explained to us.

One thing the revolution has always done is explain things to those who don't fully understand. In that sense, Fidel has been a patient teacher, concerning himself with reaching even the least informed citizen. That's why people say Fidel is an educator, and it's true. He's a master at helping people understand. And people have seen that his ideas correspond to reality. That is why they trust him. When he explained why we couldn't let ourselves be inspected, why we could neither give in nor give up, the people understood.

Che was right when he said an entire people was prepared to sacrifice themselves. It didn't matter that the enemy had nuclear weapons, or that it had the military might it did. That has never really mattered to us. When I think back on those days, and with the degree of military training I now have, I realize that we truly had great courage, great determination, great bravery. This is what has always forced the enemy to stop and think. When a people is determined to defend itself, no weapon can defeat them. Fidel has said moral weapons can be more powerful than nuclear weapons. José Martí said the same thing: "trenches of ideas are stronger than trenches of stone." The Cuban revolution has eloquently proven the truth of Martí's assertion.

WATERS: That was the decisive factor in the resolution of the October Crisis. It was not Kennedy and Khrushchev who decided the outcome. It was the Cuban people. Kennedy and his advisers understood what was happening here in Cuba.

11 Following the October 1962 missile crisis, the U.S. government, with Soviet acquiescence, demanded that the United Nations conduct an "inspection" of Cuba to verify that the Soviet nuclear missiles were being withdrawn. Cuba unambiguously refused this demand. Cuba's position was expressed by Fidel Castro on October 23, 1962: "Anyone who tries to come and inspect Cuba should know that he will have to come ready for battle."

VILLEGAS: I think those two historical moments—the October Crisis and Girón—were decisive in consolidating the revolution. And the attitude and character of Fidel during both events was decisive. We can't imagine a struggle without someone in charge, and Fidel has always led. Che talked about this, about why Fidel is so important.

Fidel led the troops at Girón. He got there, although our people didn't want him to be there. But he knew it was important not only to command those who were going to fight, but to go himself to fight along with them. And the people knew he was there. This gave each combatant extraordinary moral courage, to know their commander was there with them. That he hadn't just given them orders, but was sharing their fate. That was decisive.

The decision during the October Crisis that under no conditions would we accept being inspected was also important. There was no fear during either of these two events. We were fully convinced we were right and would triumph. Just like we're convinced now that we are right and that, sooner rather than later, we'll win, we'll overcome the situation we're in.

WATERS: How did the working people respond when the October Crisis ended? How did they view the settlement between Washington and Moscow?

VILLEGAS: The response was one of great unity. It wasn't a matter of not knowing the risks. The Cuban people were fully aware of the risks. We also knew that to give in entailed even greater risks. We maintained the same stance as our leaders.

The strong identification between Fidel and the people—which continues today—meant that everyone understood and supported the position of our government. For that reason, some of us didn't understand the Soviets. The vast majority of Cubans never understood why the Soviets caved in.

I've read some of the analyses that have been made of the crisis. In truth, the Soviets did not have their feet on the ground, because at the time their intercontinental nuclear weapons capability was extremely low. The relationship of forces was totally against them. The North Americans had much greater capacity in intercontinental weapons. That's why the Soviets brought their weapons here.

But we didn't expect the Soviets to back down. For the Cuban people, who are well-informed, it was a great disillusionment that they backed down. We had the image of the Soviets from World War II, men of sacrifice, effort, courage. The general image was one of warmth and respect.

Our decision to stand firm, to not back down, was understood perfectly by the people. Later they didn't understand why the Soviets hadn't maintained the same position we had. That's the truth.

Social aims of the Rebel Army

WATERS: I'd like to go back to the early days of the revolution and your experiences as a young soldier under Che's command at La Cabaña.[12] There is a very specific thing related to culture and education, to the social aims of the Rebel Army, that we'd like to ask you about.

One of the recent "biographies" of Che quotes from some dispatches sent by U.S. embassy personnel to Washington during the first months of 1959. The communiqués express concern over what was happening in the garrison at La Cabaña. Che, they reported, was doing something with very disturbing implications. He was organizing a department of culture within the Rebel Army and teaching soldiers to read! The Department of Culture was also doing things like organizing concerts, poetry readings, and ballet performances right there in La Cabaña, not for the officers but for all the soldiers. The dispatch said this was very worrisome, because it showed

12 Located in Havana, La Cabaña had been a garrison of the dictatorship's army before the revolution. On the evening of January 2–3, 1959, Guevara's column took over La Cabaña, and he became commander of the Rebel Army base stationed in the fort. The Batista regime's main garrisons were soon closed by the revolution and converted into schools.

Che's communist tendencies.[13]

I think this captures something very important, on both sides. The U.S. government had good reason to be afraid, of course. When education and the cultural conquests of all previous civilization become the property of the working class, when working people take this as their right, their prerogative, the rulers should tremble. A new ruling class is in the process of asserting itself. The incident also captures the importance that not only Che but the entire leadership of the Rebel Army gave to education, to broadening the cultural horizons of working people. It captures the class character . . .

VILLEGAS: . . . of the revolution.

WATERS: Yes, and the aspirations of working people to transform themselves, to educate themselves, to be the bearers of culture into the future that they alone can build.

VILLEGAS: Che felt that the task of creating and developing the Rebel Army's Department of Instruction and Culture at the time was not only to encourage the creation of cultural works. Che was the first one to start a campaign for literacy. Because there is no culture without literacy.

The Rebel Army was an army of people with humble origins. If you read the book *Secretos de generales,* you'll see that almost all the generals interviewed come from families of workers or peasants. That was the composition of the Rebel Army. That's why the first thing we did was set up schools to eradicate illiteracy. The Department of Instruction was created, and everyone who couldn't read and write was enrolled in these schools. Che looked for teachers and the work began.

As part of all this, a movement was created to bring cultural works to those who had never seen them before, to the members of the Rebel Army. We had a large theater in La

13 The dispatch, dated March 20, 1959, is quoted on page 152 of Jorge Castañeda's biography of Guevara, *Compañero: The Life and Death of Che Guevara* (New York: Alfred A. Knopf, 1997).

Cabaña, a huge theater that could hold the entire garrison. Plays were put on there, ballet performances, and other cultural presentations. Movies were brought in, and other compañeros would join us for discussion after a movie was shown. The purpose of all this was to raise the cultural level of the army, which at that time was very low. Almost all of us were peasants.

I think the North Americans must have been worried, thinking that culture for workers and peasants was a sign of communism. But our purpose was to create a movement that later grew very powerful in the army, with the aim of becoming participants in culture, making it our own. So a group of amateurs developed, which put on plays, performed songs, held festivals. All these things were promoted as part of the process of creating a higher cultural level.

We are still fighting for this today. In the armed forces we're still fighting for soldiers not to become isolated. Because the life of a military man ends up isolating him from cultural events unless that is consciously combated. For example, I can tell you that one of the hardest things we face in the army is to get soldiers into the habit of going to museums from time to time. You've got to take people there. Soldiers don't spontaneously go to museums very often. The soldier has very little free time, and when he does he looks for other forms of entertainment. We're fighting hard for this, to get people used to going to museums, to have culture become ingrained in the military environment, to maintain a cultural level, to get people to like cultural events, to like poetry, to like theater. But also for them to be able to know when the poetry is not good, to be able to appreciate the quality of cultural works.

Che was a man with a very high cultural level. He was not just someone with a broad political knowledge. He also had broad cultural knowledge. He liked poetry, the theater, all these things, and he tried to get all of us to take part in it.

Today the entire population has a different cultural level. The Special Period, of course, has meant fewer performances being opened, but now we're beginning to see a resurgence. We have real theater, like the Escambray Theater Company,[14] which brings plays directly to the countryside, and it's met a tremendous response.

There's an element of truth in what the North Americans were saying about this. Nobody writes or produces a play for the sole purpose of educating people about theater. In other countries, people usually do it for money. But in the case of the revolution, it wasn't for economic reasons. The important thing was getting the message across. Culture enables man to be fuller, more complete, more human, and therefore more revolutionary.

I can tell you, for example, that I worked on *Mother* when I was in the school for administrators, and we presented that play.[15] Shortly thereafter we organized a theater competition at school, and we put on a number of plays.

So that's the assignment Che was given at that time, and I think he carried it out extraordinarily well. He developed a series of initiatives that were very good.

Later he founded a magazine, *Verde Olivo,* which many people followed because of its clear message from a political and cultural standpoint. It was a weekly of the armed forces directed very much to the entire population.

At the time, when the party had not yet acquired a mass size, the armed forces was the most authentic representative of the people's interests, of the interests of the workers. That was where you found the best of the country's working people. The people trusted the armed forces, and they still do. Fidel once said, and Raúl repeats it every day, that the Rebel Army is the soul of the revolution. Raúl says the armed forces continue to be the soul of the revolution. And it is true. The people

14 The Escambray theater group, based in a rural area of Cuba's Escambray mountains, is one of Cuba's best-known. For thirty years it has staged plays in towns and villages across Cuba, including the most isolated areas.
15 *Mother,* written in 1906 by the Russian writer Maxim Gorky, recounts the struggle of working people under tsarism in the years before 1917.

see the armed forces as the representative of the revolution.

Of course, there are still a lot of people who were among the original founders of the armed forces, people of very humble origins. Raúl has been at the helm of the armed forces, and this has guaranteed that they do not go off track. Raúl is a very strict person; very fair, but he demands that those serving under him be held accountable for their errors. The people have tremendous trust in the armed forces.

WATERS: The policy on education and culture that Che put in practice at La Cabaña was not his policy but the policy of the revolution. It was first implemented by the Rebel Army in the Sierra, wasn't it?

VILLEGAS: Yes, Fidel and Che began it in the Sierra. As the guarantor of the revolution, the Rebel Army had to raise the educational and cultural level of the people. That's where the literacy campaign began. Then it was extended to the entire population. But it started with the Rebel Army.

Revolutionary Armed Forces

WATERS: Your remarks concerning the trust the Cuban people have in the armed forces makes me think about what is occurring now in Nicaragua, Honduras, and Guatemala, the terrible social disaster unfolding there following Hurricane Mitch.[16] It is useful to contrast this with the way the Cuban government responded when Hurricane Georges swept across Cuba a few weeks earlier. The armed forces took emergency measures, mobilized resources to help evacuate people and livestock and protect property. The kind of social disaster occurring in Cen-

16 The fall of 1998 saw two major hurricanes devastate the Caribbean and Central America.

   Hurricane Georges slammed into the Caribbean in September 1998, killing over 300 people in Puerto Rico, Haiti, and the Dominican Republic. In Cuba, although the storm damaged 40,000 homes, because of the civil defense evacuations, the death toll was held to six.

   Hurricane Mitch hit Central America in November, killing over 9,000 people, mostly in Honduras and Nicaragua.

tral America would be inconceivable in Cuba, because the government and armed forces represent the same class interests as the big majority of the people.

VILLEGAS: In Guatemala, they are criticizing the president, among other things, for not going to the areas affected by the catastrophe. Compare this with what happened here during Hurricane Flora in 1963, which was one of the most powerful hurricanes ever to hit Cuba. Over the objections of the rest of the national leadership, Fidel was right there in the middle of the storm, putting himself at risk and nearly drowning. He was riding an armored transport vehicle and traveling aboard a helicopter, evacuating children. You can understand why the people of this country love Fidel so much.

This time he didn't go there himself, but you saw him on television, not sleeping day or night, following the status of the hurricane, keeping people informed about what was happening. He sent Raúl to the eastern provinces, however, as well as Machadito and Balaguer.[17] And knowing Fidel, I imagine that he was calling them on the phone every hour asking how things were going and getting information. He couldn't sit still at all, knowing he wasn't there on the front lines. But he made absolutely sure someone was there on the spot at all times, to say what had to be done to prevent damage. His direct instructions were that the party had to remain there on the scene. And the president, Fidel personally, was the one who was seeing to what had to be done, down to the last detail—how to prevent electric power lines from falling, how to guarantee that the people maintained discipline.

KOPPEL: What role did the FAR play in these mobilizations?

VILLEGAS: The FAR helped out with helicopters, with armored transport vehicles, with the presidents of the Civil Defense units, who in Cuba report to the FAR and its minister. The head of Civil Defense is a deputy minister of the armed

17 José Ramón Machado Ventura (Machadito) and José Ramón Balaguer are members of the Political Bureau of the Communist Party of Cuba.

forces. So there's a direct link. When the general staff is acti-
vated in a municipality, you're actually activating the entire
defense apparatus that we have in each of these regions, but
for specific purposes, such as combating hurricanes, disasters,
things like that. It's not like in the past when we would have
to go and evacuate people. Now the population is more organized under the leadership of the Civil Defense, which is part
of the armed forces. Our participation, the participation of the
FAR itself, is less public, but it's more a leadership role. You
also have the party and all the other institutions. When necessary, all the troops participate too. It must be remembered that
the Revolutionary Armed Forces are the people in uniform.

WATERS: This broad leadership role of the FAR has always
been very important in Cuba. After the events with Ochoa,
Abrantes, and the others, Fidel called on the top leadership
of the armed forces to take on even more responsibilities.
That's when Furry [Abelardo Colomé] became minister of the
interior, I believe.

VILLEGAS: Yes, after the Abrantes affair.

WATERS: A year ago Division General Ulises Rosales del
Toro, who was Raúl's second at the time, took over as minister of the sugar industry. Turning around sugar production is
undoubtedly one of the most difficult challenges the country
faces. Fidel often makes these kinds of demands on the leadership of the FAR. It's one of the differences with the top
officer corps of imperialist armies. When they retire from active duty, with very lucrative business connections, they often become millionaires. The generals of the FAR exemplify
the place of the army in Cuban society. They take on the tough-
est jobs, winning people's respect.

What has been the role of the armed forces in the Special
Period, and how is the army responding to the more difficult
material conditions Cuba has faced in recent years?

VILLEGAS: Through its example the FAR is helping to solve a
whole series of tasks. Because of the confidence people have

in the army, as you were saying, whenever there's a need for a cadre who is a real sharpshooter, eyes turn to members of the FAR. That explains the example of Ulises, due to the situation we currently face with sugar.

Members of the armed forces are trained to provide an example of austerity, of honesty, of honor. Moreover, they are people who know how to lead. And that's extremely important. In a factory, an enterprise, an institution, you are leading human beings. That's why you need organizational ability—to be able to lead people. And this plays a big role in decisions to take cadres out of the armed forces and put them in such positions.

Fidel said something recently that's a source of pride for us: we don't have anyone from the armed forces who is rich. No member of the armed forces has utilized that position to get rich. Rather, every member of the armed forces who leaves does so under such extraordinarily humble circumstances that they have to look for another job in order to continue paying their bills. Because there are no privileges in our armed forces, no one who retires has privileges other Cubans don't.

What we receive is honor and recognition from the people for the work, the effort, and the sacrifice we've made in defense of the country. When I retire, in my neighborhood, the CDRs will throw a party for me. In recognition of my work they will read a summary of my biography, and that's it. What the members of the armed forces need are incentives of a moral character. That doesn't mean our material needs are completely neglected. We still get a wage that you can pretty much get by on, although I wouldn't say it's easy now in the Special Period. Many who retire have to look for work in other places, and they keep working. They're still in good health, they have a lot of experience, and this enables them to continue feeling useful. We're also not accustomed to being idle. That's something we don't like. We like to always be doing something.

But among all the retirees from the armed forces, you won't

find anyone who's gotten rich, anyone who's misused the position they've had in the armed forces. And if they're given leadership tasks, it's because of their ability from a leadership and administrative standpoint, because they have experience in leading others.

What a military person needs most, I think, is recognition by society. For example, currently, whenever people see things going badly, someone will ask, "Why don't they bring a military person here?" It's completely different from other countries. Camilo [Cienfuegos] once said the Rebel Army is the people in uniform. And it's no different today in the slightest. That statement by Camilo still holds up. It's a great truth.

WATERS: Many readers of the *Militant* and *Perspectiva Mundial* read with great pleasure the interviews with generals López Cuba, Carreras, and Fernández that were published a few months ago. A comrade in Pittsburgh, Pennsylvania, a major steel-producing center in the United States, read them together with some of his coworkers who he said were very impressed. When I asked, "What is it that impressed you and your fellow workers about the interviews?" the answer was very interesting. After thinking a few seconds, he replied, "Two things. First of all, the political level of those generals." We're used to the fact that Fidel's speeches are very political, he said, but these interviews show there's a much broader political leadership cadre. He noted that generals in the United States are not thought of as being men of profound ideas.

The second thing that impressed him and his coworkers, he said, was "the humanity of the generals."

Don't those two observations capture important leadership qualities, political qualities, that distinguish a revolutionary army?

Political education

VILLEGAS: The political level of a general, of a soldier in our armed forces cannot be compared with that in a capitalist army.

Indian Swaad℠
Taste of India

Indian Swaad ***(Taste of India)***

Citigroup Center
Ogilvie Metra Train Station (Food Court)
500 West Madison Street
Chicago, IL 60661
(312) 993-1019

We Invite You to Try our Authentic Indian Cuisines

FREE SAMOSA

WITH A PURCHASE OF AN ENTREE MEAL

(In-Store Purchase Only, Coupon Required)

www.IndianSwaad.com

Because the capitalist army claims to be nonpolitical, while we are a political army. We are fully aware that we are a political army. And we're fully aware of what we are defending.

To give this awareness a theoretical foundation, we study. There is a thorough program of political education. We don't just educate ourselves militarily, at the military academy. A certain percentage of our officers have also graduated from the Ñico López School,[18] and have gotten their degree there, at the party school. They have a degree in political science or social science. This always gives you a different way of looking at questions, to always see them from a political standpoint, as a Marxist and a Leninist.

In the military academy, we have our political specializations. But within the armed forces, there is a political education system, in which the generals and the combatants participate.

In the army a series of lectures are given, for example, that take place every semester, lasting three days. In the Western Army, government ministers and university professors are brought to speak on specific topics.

When we take the case of globalization, for example, we look at it from different angles. How the development of the productive forces led to globalization, as Marx explained. How, as Fidel has said, it is an inevitable process that will either be socialist or capitalist. How neoliberal globalization is capitalist globalization. We look at how it affects international communications, the influence of the Internet, the information superhighway, all those things.

That is one example, but we also have classes in Martí, in Marx, in Lenin. Twice a month there are classes with eight hours of instruction. There are also classes for rank-and-file soldiers, an entire system. But we don't leave it there. We also give classes to workers, to civilians.

18 The advanced-level school of the Communist Party of Cuba, named after a veteran of the Moncada attack and *Granma* expedition.

The subject matter in the courses given in the army is recorded and taken to all the units. Lectures given by ministers, by leaders of the revolution, are recorded on video and later shown to all the units. The course material on a number of subjects from the perspective of the ideas of Marx, Lenin, and Martí, are collected together in a notebook. Last year the topics dealt primarily with Che. We analyzed all aspects of Che's ideas.

We also have a system for studying anniversary dates. We have what are called "encounters with history." These require real preparation. In the Western Army, for example, on August 13 we study "an analysis of Fidel's political-military thought."[19] On that date we have a discussion on the different aspects of Fidel's ideas. Each basic party unit has to assign a team to research a particular aspect of Fidel's ideas and then give a presentation to the soldiers. The party unit has to approve the presentation beforehand—that is, the group of communists studies it collectively. They add to it, delete from it, and enrich it. This is also a part of political education.

KOPPEL: In the last year or so, we've noted the activities that veteran leaders of the FAR like yourself and other compañeros have been promoting, above all in meetings with young people in workplaces, in schools, in universities, in the community.

VILLEGAS: This is very interesting work. We call it patriotic-military-internationalist work. In recent years, as a result of the Special Period, it has fallen to the armed forces to make sure this work doesn't drop off, but is kept up. The goal is to cultivate the historic, combative traditions of our people. Five years ago, the Association of Combatants of the Revolution was created. It is the only veterans' organization, composed of three generations of Cubans encompassing various struggles for the defense of the revolution: the Rebel Army, the struggle

19 Fidel Castro was born on August 13, 1926.

against bandits and Playa Girón, and internationalists. It also includes active-duty members of both the armed forces and the Ministry of the Interior. Anyone with fifteen years active duty should belong, or can belong.

I said "should" because automatically, when the association learns that someone has fifteen years, we invite them to join the Association of Combatants of the Revolution. Members are given a schedule of activities in schools, with children, teaching about our combative traditions. This is important, because it's not just someone talking about a battle that took place many years ago. In most cases it's the combatants themselves telling children about what happened on a historic date. It's living history. For example, I am assigned to the school right here at the corner. I have been asked to go and meet with the students, to make a presentation about the meaning of the revolution's triumph, the Rebel Army, and then open it up for questions. It's another one of the methods we have of patriotic and internationalist education.

In a general sense, the party leads this work. It's the most concrete form of conducting ideological work among the people. Military law—I think it's Article 75—says that patriotic-military and internationalist education is political work carried out among the population with the aim of defending the revolution. Why do we say "with the aim of defending the revolution"? Because we're creating a sense of patriotism, we're creating a spirit of defense of the homeland based in all our traditions and values.

KOPPEL: During the Special Period, the economic measures Cuba has been obliged to adopt have brought greater penetration of the world capitalist market and its values and social relations, which are the antithesis of the social relations and values the revolution has fought for. Revolutionaries in Cuba are waging a political battle against all these influences. What impact does this situation have on the type of living history you convey and the political lessons you try to bring to a generation of young people who have never been through the experience of making a socialist revolution and beginning to build a new society?

Union of Young Communists

VILLEGAS: I believe what we're doing is vitally important. By itself, it doesn't solve the problem of the ideological struggle. There are a whole series of institutions that must also be a part of this fight, the whole ideological fight. But having people who are respected, who are highly regarded in their own neighborhoods, who are examples of sacrifice, work, and dedication, has a deep influence on young people.

I think the Union of Young Communists (UJC) should have more of a presence in the neighborhoods. Not only in the factories, not only in the schools, but in the neighborhoods too. Sometimes a young person is not in school and not working, yet he or she is in the neighborhood. We can't leave them on their own like that, unattached. That's my opinion.

The party has neighborhood nuclei or cells, but the UJC doesn't. It has cells in the factories, the schools, the armed forces. Yet youth are the most numerous group of "unattached" people in the neighborhoods. In the Western Army, the UJC pays attention to nonmembers.

The UJC has formed the Panchito Gómez Toro Youth Brigades. It's a voluntary organization. In fact, to emphasize that it's voluntary, everyone who joins has to pay twenty cents. Members can participate in recreational activities and other events. Among them are UJC members who carry out recruitment work talking about what the UJC is, talking about our revolutionary history. UJC members get paired up with nonmembers. We say to a UJC member: "You look after so-and-so, pay attention to him, work with her." We have to do something similar with our youth who are neither in school nor working. We can't just ignore them, just leave them for the enemy to influence. If they like North American music, if they like dancing and things like that, we have to see to it that they have a life too. When I was young, I was a Boy Scout. I played volleyball, baseball. I had a series of activities that led me to have a healthy life.

Healthy activity has to be available to the youth. And it has to be organized without telling them what to do. Note that the Panchito Gómez Toro Youth Brigades are a separate group; it's not the UJC. A UJC member creates the group, organizes it, and UJC members join, but it doesn't belong to the UJC. They have to win their influence individually, as members of this organization, this brigade that encompasses almost everyone. Whatever influence they have, that's the influence of the UJC. There's no help from the local UJC committee, saying "you must do this." No. The local UJC committee carries out this work through its members who belong to the brigade. It has to guide its members in how to win over other young people to their ideas. Because unless you do so, you kill the spirit of participation by the youth. You have to win them over.

WATERS: Where does the name "Panchito Gómez Toro" come from? Who was he?

VILLEGAS: Panchito Gómez Toro was a son of Máximo Gómez. He died fighting with Maceo. He's a symbol of Cuban youth, his story is a very beautiful one. He traveled with Martí through Latin America and was greatly influenced by Martí and Maceo. When Maceo fell, Panchito went to defend Maceo's body and was killed.

Che and the Congo revolutionary war

WATERS: In the last year some parts of Che's *Episodes of the Congo Revolutionary War* have been published here in Cuba. There have also been a number of articles in the Cuban press, including one that you wrote, about the internationalist mission to the Congo, which had previously been a little-known chapter in the history of Africa and in the history of the Cuban revolution.[20]

20 See glossary notes, Congo revolutionary war.

VILLEGAS: Yes, I'm also preparing the diary I wrote in the Congo during this time.

WATERS: There's a lot of commentary, especially by enemies of the Cuban revolution, who say Cuba's effort to aid the liberation forces in the Congo was a total disaster, an adventure. This type of criticism appears in several of the recent biographies of Che and in other articles. What is your evaluation?

VILLEGAS: I think we have to view the events in the Congo from two sides: the political and the human.

First the human side. During Che's last trip through Africa and Asia between December 1964 and March 1965, he was able to evaluate the revolutionary potential in Africa, and consider how the Cuban revolution could help realize that potential. He proposed to Fidel that Cuba assist some of those African countries, such as Guinea, Angola, and the Congo. And Fidel believed this was correct.

At the same time, Che himself had already made his decision to leave Cuba. He had not decided to go to Africa—anyone who thinks so is completely mistaken. Che wanted to go to Argentina, to his homeland, to fight for Latin America. But the conditions for this did not yet exist. So he was asked to postpone these plans for a little while. It was to be a brief postponement, and he felt he could use that time to help the Africans. Not as a combatant, but as an adviser.

Everything—including the information from compañeros who had been sent there earlier—indicated that suitable conditions existed. Che studied the situation in Mozambique, Guinea, and Angola, but it turned out that the Congo was really the place with the most battle-tested fighters, with more of a tradition of struggle, with the whole Lumumba experience behind them. We should add that Che admired and felt a certain degree of commitment toward Lumumba and his legacy. Che was really inclined to try to help Lumumba's people above all.

That wasn't the whole story. The decision wasn't just for

Che and his unit to go to Africa. The Cuban government also followed through with all the other commitments made during Che's trip. A group of Cubans, a battalion of troops, was sent to the French Congo to help. A group was also sent to Guinea. In other words, the commitments made were not left hanging.[21]

With the decision that Che would go, Víctor Dreke, who had earlier been chosen to lead the Congo group, was named second in command. Everyone in the unit was black; the only whites were Che—who was going for a short period of time, to assist—and his liaison with Latin America, José María Martínez Tamayo, Papi.

It was thought that white combatants would not be accepted by the revolutionary organizations in Africa. That's why, Che and Papi aside, all the rest of the Cubans were black.

Once we got to the Congo, we found that things weren't at all like we had been told by the leaders there. For one thing, we thought that [Laurent] Kabila and [Gaston] Soumialot, the leaders of the struggle in that region, would leave their centers in exile and come join us at the front.[22] That didn't happen. The leaders didn't come join us. This was the situation when Che got there, and it didn't change.

We had made commitments, and we followed through with them, including sending doctors and others to help. Che had Fidel's complete backing. Fidel said, "We're going to support Che in whatever way we can." He sent a number of leading people who might help the organization of the struggle, including [Oscar] Fernández Mell, [Oscar Fernández] Padilla for the Cuban embassy in Tanzania, [Emilio] Aragonés.

If a criticism can be made, I think it's that we didn't fully

21 Following Guevara's trip, Cuban volunteers were sent to assist liberation fighters in a number of African countries, including Guinea-Bissau, Mozambique, the Congo-Brazzaville (the former French Congo), and Angola.
22 Laurent Kabila and Gaston Soumialot were two leaders of the movement identified with Lumumba.

understand the characteristics and traditions of the Africans we worked with at that time. The ranks accepted us, but their leaders didn't. That's the reality. It wasn't the fault of any individual; it was a question of leadership traditions.

At a certain point, Che decided that any Cuban who wanted to leave should go, while he and those who wanted would stay, because he saw the possibilities of cadres developing among the fighters themselves.

Che's conviction was always that the struggle sifts out its own leaders. The struggle itself reveals who is willing and able to be a leader, and who is not. Che saw that among that group of thousands of men, their own leaders would emerge. He worked hard to find someone who would share that responsibility together with him. But in the end, he wasn't successful. He was unsuccessful, in my opinion, because there was not yet a deep enough sense of nationhood among them.

Those who had such a consciousness were not there at the front. Instead, there was a tribal consciousness, a regional consciousness. A sense of nationhood had not yet established roots. This, in my opinion, is the reason for the failure.

From the personal standpoint, Che was torn during the period he was in Africa. He wanted to leave Cuba to collaborate with other fighters. He was unable to go to Argentina. So he decided to go where he felt he could be a help. His admiration, his esteem, the regard he felt for Lumumba, for those people in struggle, who really had considerable forces, weighed heavily. But the fundamental problem there, which he couldn't surmount, was tribal divisions. It was the lack of identification among the different groups. At its roots, it was a problem of social development.

We managed to get around the divisions to some degree by putting a group of Cubans to work with each tribe. Then they had something in common—the Cubans who were advising them. This allowed Che to exercise leadership. Although people didn't speak the same language, although they couldn't understand each other, they more or less always had a link, because there were Cubans among them. This was the link that connected all of them to a leadership, and at certain moments it allowed everyone to work together.

But there was something we could not do, as a matter of principle: go around the leadership that invited us there. It's a complex thing. We could not pull everyone around us without dealing with Soumialot, Kabila, and the others, who didn't join us at the front.

Therefore, up to the last moment we remained loyal to them. If one could say there was an error in going to the aid of the Congo struggle, one has to look at it from the standpoint of what we were attempting to achieve.

We were trying to organize them in a way that would help them develop the struggle much more broadly. This was Che's conception. And help them in whatever way possible. Our idea was not to make them communists, not to make them socialists. The idea was to help establish Lumumba's ideas and what he had been fighting for. As could be expected, our influence moved them a little to the left, made them more anti-imperialist, helped tie them to the most progressive ideas. And we were making progress in this.

WATERS: You could not know what was possible, what could be accomplished, without trying. It would be decided in struggle.

VILLEGAS: The fact is, we came smack up against reality: we had no leaders on whom we could lean for support.

A decision was made by the forces in the Congo to initiate combat at Front de Force.[23] It was done precipitously, before things were ready. More preparation and training were needed. In irregular warfare, if you do the basics, things can go well. But we had to start from zero.

23 On June 29, 1965, a guerrilla unit composed of fighters from Cuba and Rwanda led an unsuccessful attack on a mercenary garrison at Front de Force (also known as Force Bendera) in the Congo. Fourteen Rwandans and four Cubans were killed in the battle.

We were up against ideological and religious concepts, a very complicated task. "Let's dig a trench," you might say. And the response would be, "No, we're not getting in. Holes in the ground are for the dead." You might say, "You can't shoot that way, you have to aim the rifle." But it's not just aiming. We had to show them how to close one eye and use a directing eye. We had to teach them how to close one eye, because there were some who didn't know how. All this required that we train them first, and for this great patience was needed.

You don't see these things in Che's book; what you see in it is a dialogue taking place based around the day's events. And when someone is as critical as Che, the things written down are always harsh, especially when things are going unfavorably.

Our group of Cubans still had many compañeros with a sixth-grade education. It was a challenge to understand the Africans' customs, behavior, and life. This situation led some people—not very many, two or three—to ask to leave and return to Cuba.

Che could not grasp this. You have to understand what being a Cuban revolutionary meant to Che. He always had a very high standard—like everyone holds today. Che believed that a Cuban revolutionary, above all, had to be consistent in word and deed.

First, there was his understanding of what it meant to be a revolutionary. A revolutionary, he once said, is "the highest level the human species achieves." But then he added the adjective "Cuban" to it. As he says in his letter to Fidel,[24] he would never renounce being a Cuban revolutionary. Following Che's lead, other Cubans there felt the same way. Che's dedication, his selflessness—these qualities are not easy for each and every individual to achieve. When someone representing the Cuban revolution did not act in a way consistent with these qualities, Che became extremely critical of them.

24 See López Cuba interview, page 42.

You'd have to have lived through this to understand it. I often think I'm not really getting across when I try to explain it. And when I explain the conditions there, I don't do so just to defend Che. I'm speaking about reality. And our time there was very short, transitory.

WATERS: At the beginning you said there were two sides, the political and the human. What about the political?

VILLEGAS: Seen from the angle of world politics, the situation was very complex. We were on the continent of Africa, in a world that was much less globalized than it is today. There were organized regional groupings that pursued their own continental interests.

After combat began at the battle of Front de Force, in which we lost some fighters, Che decided to move to guerrilla warfare. We began to conduct ambushes and to utilize methods of irregular warfare, carrying out guerrilla attacks.

The government of the Congo, against which the Lumumba movement was fighting, appealed to the Organization of African Unity, requesting that the OAU intervene in this war because of the presence of Cubans. There were discussions within the OAU and among the African presidents at a meeting in Accra, and they adopted a general line of not giving assistance to opposition forces in any domestic conflict.[25] They decided they would only support forces fighting against a colonial power. This meant that in the future they would give support only to revolutionary movements in the Portuguese colonies—the only colonies that remained. This was a change from the previous position of the OAU, which had given open support to the pro-Lumumba forces.

Of course there was Namibia too, but it was not seen as a colony. It was supposedly held in trusteeship by the UN.

The Congo groups weren't fighting directly against a colo-

25 Meeting in Accra, Ghana, October 21–26, 1965, the Organization of African Unity decided to limit military aid by foreign powers.

nial power. Formally the Congo was independent; the old colonial power, Belgium, was gone. They were fighting their own brothers, even if the government forces were representatives of colonial and imperialist powers, the exploiters. It was a different situation, a struggle against Mobutu. And it was portrayed as if the two sides were massacring each other.

The OAU also exerted pressure on the revolutionary movement in the Congo, forcing them to say that outside forces had to leave. Pressure was put on Mobutu—actually Mobutu was gone at this point, Joseph Kasavubu was in—to get all the forces there to leave, and to get the mercenaries out. In this context, they also pressured Tanzania to confiscate the ships, weapons, and other matériel destined for the pro-Lumumba movement forces.

WATERS: The whole history of Africa would have been different if the conditions in the Congo had more closely resembled what you had originally thought.

VILLEGAS: It would have been completely different if, apart from the conditions I explained earlier concerning the individual leaders, the basis had been laid to keep fighting. The presence of small groups of Cubans in each unit made this possible. So when this new political situation developed, Fidel left open the final decision. Fidel gave Che a free hand; Che himself would decide what to do. And he would always have Cuba's support. A senior delegation from the [Communist Party] Central Committee was sent from Cuba for discussions with the Tanzanians.

But the problem was with the OAU agreement. It wasn't a problem with the Tanzanians.

Che tried, he fought, he worked to see who would stay. He told the Cubans, "Whoever wants to leave can leave. Whoever wants to stay can stay." That was the decision he took. Still, not a single leader of the groups that were fighting in the Congo joined us on the front lines. Not one. At this point the idea arose of going in search of Pierre Mulele at the other end of the country. We ourselves started to exert pressure by saying that the logical thing would be to go in search of Mulele.

Che told us to go look for Mulele. But we would have had to cross all of the Congo, a country of something like three million square kilometers. Crossing it would have involved a journey like Mao Zedong's Long March. That was his idea. Che wanted to go with four others. But we argued: How could Che know for sure that Mulele would be there at the front, that he was at the head of his fighters, given that Soumialot and Kabila hadn't come to the front. That made Che think. He really had no basis to be sure that Mulele would be found there, after this gigantic march. That was when he decided to leave the Congo.

I truly believe that Che's position, if we look at it from an individual point of view, was an example of selflessness. He subordinated himself completely, without any conditions. Most never realized who he was.[26] And when the leaders realized Che was there, it was very disconcerting for them. What should they do? They themselves had never been there at the front of their troops. They hadn't shown any interest in being there. And now someone had come to help them inside the country, while they were outside. This was a really difficult situation for them. By the time they were faced with this decision, the OAU pressure had already begun, demanding that we get out.

So you have to take into account the time and the place in which all this occurred. In the few brief months he was there, Che gradually realized there were no prospects for the thing to go anywhere.

Revolution's reinforcement detachment

WATERS: Last year, the remains of Che and several of the other compañeros who died in Bolivia were returned to Cuba.[27]

26 During his seven months in the Congo, Guevara took the nom de guerre Tatu, and was not publicly identified as leader of the Cuban contingent. Only a few leaders of the Congo liberation forces learned his true identity.
27 See López Cuba interview, page 36.

You commanded the military honor guard for the solemn and impressive ceremony in Santa Clara. What seemed to us most important about those events was that they became a vehicle for the Cuban people to express their revolutionary commitment, to reaffirm their support for the proletarian internationalist course that Che and the other compañeros in Bolivia fought for.

The immense dignity of the ceremony, the spontaneous outpouring of emotion and respect, paid homage to all those who have fought and died for humanity's future. What impact did these events have inside Cuba?

VILLEGAS: We're not a people who make a big deal when someone falls. We don't worship the dead. I think the reception for Che has a deeper political and ideological character. It's not simply respect for someone who died. It's really a show of love, of esteem, of identification with what Che represented. That's really what's behind the tribute paid to Che by our entire people.

Che helped bring this about by what he taught and through his personal example. That personal example had a deep impact on the people. There are some Cubans who know little more about Che than that he died. Many others wish that Che were at our side today, fighting during this difficult and complex time for our people. All this, I believe, is what led so many to turn out, not only in Santa Clara, but all along the way, in massive numbers. It was identification with his ideas and his principles.

It had a tremendous impact on me. I traveled in the jeeps that carried the remains of each of the combatants. I could see the extraordinary discipline of the people, the extraordinary organization. I can tell you that from the Plaza of the Revolution in Havana, all the way to Santa Clara, there were hardly any open spaces. The people came from towns a long way from the highway to pay tribute to him.

There were some very moving things. I remember when we were entering the province of Villa Clara, for example. I don't know how they were able to get so many people there. As we passed through, they sang Carlos Puebla's song.[28] They kept singing, it was played over loudspeakers, and the people were humming along. And it was endless, endless, endless. It was deeply moving.

Fidel's brief speech at the Santa Clara ceremony was a masterpiece. It shows why he has such an impact on our people. The thoughts on people's minds were summed up by Fidel when he said that this wasn't a farewell to Che. We were welcoming a reinforcement detachment.

A reinforcement detachment! To fight alongside us!

And now Tania will join that detachment, meaning that women will become part of it.[29] This is important because of the decisive contribution women make to society. That is what Tania symbolizes. And along with Tania, nine other combatants will arrive to swell the ranks of the detachment, which as Fidel said is a Latin American detachment. And it is important for the entire continent to have a detachment of Latin American combatants here.

I am convinced these internationalists will give us much greater strength as we confront the struggles that lie ahead, the struggles we are waging.

Che's ideas are alive, and we're still fighting for these ideas, which he gave his life for. We're fighting today, during the Special Period, to achieve greater productivity, and to be more true to our principles. That's what these ideas mean today. They are the dreams and ideas that unite us.

---

28 Carlos Puebla was a well-known Cuban musician who wrote "Hasta siempre, Comandante," a tribute to Che Guevara that remains popular in Cuba.

29 In the closing months of 1998, the remains of ten other combatants who fought with Che Guevara were recovered in Bolivia. Among them was Haydée Tamara Bunke, known by her nom de guerre Tania, the only woman in Che's *guerrilla* in Bolivia, who fell in combat in August 1967. The remains were returned to Cuba and interred along with those of Ernesto Guevara and others at a December 30 military ceremony in Santa Clara.

Glossary notes

Abrantes, José (1933–1991) – Headed the Department of State Security for more than twenty years and served as interior minister 1985–89. He held the rank of division general in the Ministry of the Interior and was a member of the Communist Party Central Committee 1965–89. Designated Hero of the Republic of Cuba.

In July 1989 Abrantes was removed as interior minister. In August he was convicted and sentenced to twenty years in prison on charges of abuse of authority, negligence in carrying out his duties, and improper use of government funds and resources. Abrantes was replaced as minister by Army Corps General Abelardo Colomé, who at the time was deputy minister of defense and first substitute for the minister Raúl Castro.

Almeida Bosque, Juan (b. 1927) – A former bricklayer from Havana, he participated in the 1953 Moncada attack and was sentenced to ten years in prison. Released in May 1955 following a national amnesty campaign, he participated in the *Granma* expedition of November–December 1956. In February 1958 he was promoted to commander and later headed the Third Front. Almeida has carried numerous responsibilities since 1959, including head of the air force, vice minister of the FAR, and vice president of the Council of Ministers. He has been a member of the Communist Party Central Committee and Political Bureau since 1965. He is president of the National Directorate of the Association of Combatants of the Cuban Revolution.

Annexationists – In the years before 1868 two currents, led primarily by Cuban-born plantation owners and slaveholders, opposed the revolutionary struggle for independence from Spain. These

were generally referred to as annexationists and reformists. The
annexationists favored the union of Cuba with the United States.
Most looked to the slaveholding states of the U.S. South, seeing
annexation as a way to strengthen slavery in Cuba. A smaller
group looked to the U.S. North. After the U.S. Civil War, some
opponents of slavery in Cuba were also attracted to annexation-
ism, seeing it as a means to eliminate slavery. The reformists sought
to win a certain degree of autonomy from Spain, while reforming
the plantation system based on chattel slavery in order to maintain it. Slavery was abolished in Cuba only in 1886.

Aragonés, Emilio (b. 1928) – A leader of the July 26 Movement in
Cienfuegos during the insurrectional struggle, he became its national coordinator in 1960. In March 1962 he was elected to the
National Directorate and Secretariat of the Integrated Revolutionary Organization (ORI). He was a member of the Communist
Party's Central Committee 1965–91. In September 1965 he participated in a delegation sent to the Congo by the top leadership of
the party to consult and work with Che Guevara.

Balaguer, José Ramón (b. 1932) – Trained as a medical doctor, he
was involved in the clandestine struggle against the dictatorship;
joined the Rebel Army serving in the Second Eastern Front in 1958.
He has been a member of the Central Committee of the Cuban
Communist Party since 1965 and the party's Political Bureau since
1992. He is head of the Central Committee's Department of International Relations and has responsibility for the party's propaganda and educational work.

Batista, Fulgencio (1901–1973) – Former army sergeant who helped
lead a military coup by junior officers in September 1933, following a popular uprising that overturned the dictatorship of Gerardo
Machado a few weeks earlier. Batista rose to chief of staff and
increasingly became the strongman in the Junta of National Reno-
vation that emerged out of the 1933–34 revolution. As the Cuban
bourgeoisie and their Yankee patrons reconsolidated power following the initial battles of 1933, Batista bought off most of the
insurgent political leaders, using repression against those who
resisted. He remained in power until 1944, when he left office,

retaining a base of support within the army officer corps.

On March 10, 1952, Batista organized a military coup against the government headed by Authentic Party leader Carlos Prío and canceled scheduled elections. With support from Washington, Batista imposed a brutal military dictatorship. In November 1954 the Batista regime held an election to provide legal cover for the 1952 coup. The only other candidate was Ramón Grau San Martín, whose agreement to run had given legitimacy to Batista's maneuver. Grau backed out of the race the day before the election, leaving Batista the sole candidate.

Batista's regime lasted until January 1, 1959. On that day, as his military and police forces surrendered to the victorious Rebel Army advancing under the command of Fidel Castro, and as a general strike and popular insurrection spread, Batista fled the country.

Bay of Pigs – On April 17, 1961, an expeditionary force of 1,500 Cuban mercenaries invaded Cuba at the Bay of Pigs on the southern coast. The counterrevolutionaries, organized and financed by Washington, aimed to hold Cuban territory long enough to declare a provisional government that could appeal for U.S. support and direct intervention. The mercenaries, however, were defeated within seventy-two hours by Cuba's militia and Revolutionary Armed Forces. On April 19 the remaining invaders were captured at Playa Girón (Girón Beach), which is the name Cubans use to designate the battle.

Bayo, Alberto (1892–1967) – An officer in the Republican army during the Spanish civil war. In 1956 he provided military training in Mexico to the future *Granma* expeditionaries. He moved to Cuba after January 1, 1959, and worked for the Revolutionary Armed Forces. He authored a number of books on military matters, including *150 Questions for a Guerrilla*, which had been printed and circulated in several Latin American countries during the 1940s and 1950s. It was published in Havana in 1959.

Castellanos, Alberto (b. 1934) – A Rebel Army combatant in Che Guevara's column, he became part of Guevara's personal escort in 1959. In 1963–64 he volunteered for an internationalist mission in Argentina led by Jorge Ricardo Masetti. Captured in February 1964, he was imprisoned in Argentina until December 1967, never revealing his identity as a Cuban. After his release he returned to Cuba.

Castro, Fidel (b. 1926) – Born and raised in Oriente province in eastern Cuba. A student leader at the University of Havana from 1945 on. Founding member of the Orthodox Party in 1947 and central organizer of its revolutionary-minded youth. One of the party's candidates for house of representatives in the 1952 elections, which were canceled following the Batista coup. Castro led the July 26, 1953, attack on the Moncada and Bayamo garrisons and was sentenced to fifteen years in prison. His courtroom defense speech, "History Will Absolve Me," was later distributed in tens of thousands of copies across Cuba, becoming the program of the revolutionary movement. Released in May 1955 after a mass amnesty campaign, he organized the founding of the July 26 Movement a few weeks later. From Mexico, Castro prepared the *Granma* expedition, which returned to Cuba in December 1956. He commanded the Rebel Army during the 1956–58 revolutionary war. In May 1958 he became general secretary of July 26 Movement.

Castro was Cuba's prime minister from February 1959 to 1976, when he became president of the Council of State and Council of Ministers. He is commander in chief of the armed forces and has been first secretary of the Communist Party of Cuba since it was founded in 1965.

Castro, Raúl (b. 1931) – Born and raised in Oriente province in eastern Cuba. A student leader at the University of Havana, he participated in the 1953 Moncada attack and was sentenced to thirteen years in prison. He was released in May 1955 following a national amnesty campaign. A founding member of the July 26 Movement, he was a participant in the *Granma* expedition. In February 1958 he was promoted to commander and headed the Second Eastern Front.

Since October 1959 he has been minister of the Revolutionary Armed Forces. He was vice premier from 1959 until 1976, when he became vice president of the Council of State and Council of Ministers. Since 1965 he has been second secretary of the Communist Party of Cuba. He holds the rank of general of the army, the second-highest officer in the Revolutionary Armed Forces after Commander in Chief Fidel Castro.

Céspedes, Carlos Manuel de (1819–1874) – The initiator of the Cuban independence war of 1868–78 and central leader of the Republic of Cuba in Arms. See also glossary entry for Yara, Grito de.

Chibás, Eduardo (1907–1951) – A student leader of the fight against the Machado dictatorship in the 1920s and 1930s; he was founding leader of the opposition Cuban People's Party (popularly known as the Orthodox Party) in 1947 and was elected senator in 1950. As a protest against government corruption, he committed suicide in 1951 at the conclusion of a radio address.

Cienfuegos, Camilo (1932–1959) – A *Granma* expeditionary, he became a Rebel Army commander in 1958. From August to October 1958 he led a column westward from the Sierra Maestra en route to Pinar del Río. He operated in northern Las Villas province until the end of the war, working in tandem with the column led by Che Guevara based in southern Las Villas. He was named Rebel Army chief of staff following the victory over Batista in January 1959. His plane was lost at sea in October 1959 while he was returning to Havana from a mission in Camagüey to combat a counterrevolutionary mutiny led by Huber Matos.

Cienfuegos uprising – A September 5, 1957, revolt led by anti-Batista forces within the military and supported by the July 26 Movement. When the simultaneous uprisings planned for Havana and elsewhere did not occur, Batista's forces were able to rapidly crush the Cienfuegos revolt. (See *Episodes of the Cuban Revolutionary War* by Ernesto Che Guevara, the chapter "One Year of Armed Struggle.")

Cintra Frías, Leopoldo (Polo) (b. 1941) – A native of Yara, he joined the Rebel Army in November 1957, finishing the war as a lieutenant. He volunteered for internationalist missions in Angola and Ethiopia in the 1970s and headed Cuba's military mission in Angola 1983-86 and 1989. A Hero of the Republic of Cuba, he is a division general of the FAR and a member of the Political Bureau of the Communist Party of Cuba.

Colomé, Abelardo (Furry) (b. 1939) – Joined the Rebel Army in March 1957 as part of the first contingent of reinforcements sent to the Sierra Maestra by Frank País and Celia Sánchez. Served under

Fidel Castro and Raúl Castro, becoming a Rebel Army commander. In 1962–64 he volunteered for an internationalist mission in Argentina and Bolivia to prepare for and support the guerrilla front in Argentina led by Jorge Ricardo Masetti. He headed the Cuban mission in Angola during 1975–76. As army corps general, he is the third-highest-ranking Cuban military officer. He is a member of the Communist Party's Central Committee and Political Bureau, and of Cuba's Council of State. In 1984 he was designated Hero of the Republic of Cuba. He became interior minister in June 1989. Prior to that, he was deputy minister of defense and first substitute for the minister, Raúl Castro.

Committees for the Defense of the Revolution (CDRs) – Organized in 1960 on a block-by-block basis as a tool through which the Cuban people could exercise vigilance against counterrevolutionary activity. In subsequent years they have also served as a vehicle to organize participation at mass demonstrations and to take part in vaccination and other public health campaigns, civil defense, the fight against petty crime, and other civic tasks.

Communist Party of Cuba – In 1961, the July 26 Movement initiated a fusion with the Popular Socialist Party and the Revolutionary Directorate—all three of which had experienced splits and regroupment of forces as the revolution deepened—to form the Integrated Revolutionary Organizations (ORI). In 1963 it became the United Party of the Socialist Revolution; and in October 1965 the Communist Party of Cuba, with Fidel Castro as first secretary of its Central Committee.

Congo revolutionary war – From April to November 1965, Che Guevara headed a contingent of more than one hundred Cuban volunteer fighters in the eastern Congo. Harry Villegas was chief adjutant to Che in this campaign. The contingent went there to support liberation forces that belonged to the movement founded by Patrice Lumumba in their fight against the country's pro-imperialist regime.

Lumumba, principal leader of the independence movement in the former Belgian colony, and the Congo's first prime minister, was the most intransigent of the leaders resisting the efforts to keep the new nation under the thumb of imperialism. He had been ousted in September 1960 in a U.S.-backed coup led by army chief of staff Joseph Mobutu. Lumumba, who had been under the "protection" of United Nations troops, was captured and then murdered in January 1961 by imperialist-backed forces loyal to rightist figure Moise Tshombe.

In mid-1964 a new revolt broke out in the Congo led by pro-Lumumba forces. The rebels were able to gain control of Stanley-ville (today Kisangani), the country's second-largest city. They were defeated in November 1964, however, with the help of Belgian and South African mercenary forces—politically and militarily backed by Washington—whose mission was to prevent the Congo's vast mineral wealth from escaping imperialist control. Thousands were massacred as the imperialist forces retook Stanleyville.

Nevertheless, large numbers of rebel fighters remained in several areas of the country. These were the forces the Cuban volunteers assisted. In this effort, which had the official support of the Organization of African Unity (OAU), the Cuban volunteers worked together with other anti-imperialist forces in Africa, especially the revolutionary government of Ahmed Ben Bella in Algeria. In June 1965, as the Cuban volunteer contingent in the Congo was still getting established, a coup d'état in Algeria led by Houari Boumediene toppled the Ben Bella government. The coup was a major blow to revolutionary anti-imperialist forces in Africa and undermined continued support to the struggle in the Congo. In October 1965 the OAU withdrew support for the fight against the proimperialist regime. Owing to the OAU decision and deep divisions and other weaknesses among the forces in the Congo, the Cuban volunteers withdrew in November 1965.

Most fighters returned to Cuba, but Guevara, Villegas, Carlos Coello, and José María Martínez Tamayo went to Tanzania, where they remained for several months while preparations were made to open a guerrilla front in Bolivia. While in Tanzania, Guevara wrote *Episodes of the Congo Revolutionary War,* using as a reference the campaign diary he had kept. The complete manuscript, as prepared and edited by Guevara, was released in Cuba in April 1999.

Cuban Missile Crisis. See October 1962 "Missile" Crisis

Dreke, Víctor (b. 1937) – A member of the July 26 Movement in Sagua La Grande, Las Villas; he later joined the Revolutionary Directorate column that coordinated its actions with Che Guevara's Rebel Army column in the fall of 1958. Commanded forces responsible for eliminating counterrevolutionary bands in the Escambray mountains in the early 1960s. In 1965 he was second in command, under Guevara, of the Cuban volunteer contingent in the Congo. Later headed Political Directorate of the FAR.

Escambray mountains – Located in south-central Cuba. In the early 1960s, small bands of counterrevolutionaries armed and financed by Washington—popularly known in Cuba as the bandits—based themselves in the Escambray. The bandits carried out sabotage and other operations against the revolution. They were eliminated by a popular mobilization of militia units supporting operations of the Revolutionary Armed Forces.

FAR. See Revolutionary Armed Forces

Fernández Mell, Oscar (b. 1931) – A captain in Guevara's Rebel Army column, he was promoted to commander after the triumph of the revolution in 1959. In September 1965 he was part of the leadership delegation sent to the Congo by the party to consult and work with Che Guevara. A medical doctor, he later served in various posts, including head of the general staff of Cuba's Western Army, head of the general staff of the Ministry of the Revolutionary Armed Forces, and Cuba's ambassador to Britain.

Fernández Padilla, Oscar – A vice minister in the Ministry of Industry when it was headed by Che Guevara. In 1965 he took an assignment at the Cuban embassy in Tanzania, serving as liaison with the volunteer contingent in the Congo led by Guevara.

Flora, Hurricane – Slammed into Cuba in October 1963, killing more than a thousand people and causing severe economic damage.

Frías, Ciro (1928–1958) – A peasant from the Sierra Maestra, he joined the Rebel Army in January 1957. A member of Column 1, and later a captain in Column 18 in the Second Eastern Front, under the command of Raúl Castro. He was killed April 10, 1958, and was posthumously promoted to commander.

García, Guillermo (b. 1928) – A peasant from the Sierra Maestra, he was a member of a July 26 Movement cell and helped organize the regroupment of rebel forces in December 1956. He became a combatant in early 1957 in Column no. 1, and by late 1958 had been promoted to commander in the Third Eastern Front led by Juan Almeida. He has been a member of the Communist Party Central Committee since 1965 and served on the Political Bureau 1965–86. He was minister of transportation 1974–85 and is a member of the Council of State.

Girón. See Bay of Pigs

Gómez, Máximo (1836–1905) – Born in Santo Domingo (today the Dominican Republic), he was a military leader of the Cuban revolutionary armies during the 1868–78 and 1895–98 independence wars, becoming commander in chief of the independence forces in 1870. Following the defeat of Spain in 1898, he was dismissed as commander in chief of the Cuban army by the pro-imperialist regime imposed by the U.S. occupation army.

Granma – The yacht that carried eighty-two revolutionary fighters, including Fidel Castro, Raúl Castro, Ernesto Che Guevara, and Juan Almeida from Tuxpan, Mexico, to Cuba to initiate the revolutionary war against the U.S.-backed regime of Fulgencio Batista. The expeditionaries landed in southeast Cuba on December 2, 1956. *Granma* has been the name of the daily newspaper of the Communist Party of Cuba since 1965.

Guerra, Orestes (b. 1932) – A native of Yara, he joined the Rebel Army in 1957, serving in columns under the command of Fidel Castro, Che Guevara, and Camilo Cienfuegos and finishing the war as a captain. He is a brigadier general of the FAR, retired.

Guevara, Ernesto Che (1928–1967) – Argentine-born leader of the Cuban revolution. Signed on as the troop doctor in the *Granma* expedition. He was the first combatant to be promoted to the rank of commander of the Rebel Army during Cuba's revolutionary war. In late 1958 he commanded the column that captured Santa Clara, Cuba's third-largest city. Following the 1959 triumph, in addition to his military tasks, Guevara held a number of positions and responsibilities in the revolutionary government including head of the Department of Industrialization of the National Institute of Agrarian Reform (INRA), head of the National Bank, and minister of industry; he was often a spokesman for the revolutionary leadership internationally. As a leader of the July 26 Movement, he helped bring about the political regroupment that led to the founding of the Communist Party of Cuba in October 1965. In April 1965 he led the Cuban contingent that went to aid revolutionary fighters in the Congo. In late 1966 he led a vanguard detachment of internationalist volunteers to Bolivia. Wounded and captured by the Bolivian army in a CIA-organized operation on October 8, 1967, he was murdered the following day.

Hart, Armando (b. 1930) – Joined the Orthodox Youth in 1947 in Havana. He was a leader of the Revolutionary National Movement following Batista's coup. In 1955 he became a founding member of the July 26 Movement and a leader of its urban underground. He was imprisoned briefly in 1957 and escaped. He served as national coordinator of the July 26 Movement from early 1957 to January 1958, when he was captured and imprisoned on the Isle of Pines until January 1, 1959. He served as minister of education 1959–65; Communist Party organization secretary 1965–70; minister of culture 1976–97. He has been a member of the Communist Party Central Committee since 1965 and was a member of the Political Bureau 1965–86.

Hatuey – a Taino Indian chief from the island of Hispaniola (today the Dominican Republic and Haiti) who fled the Spanish colonial forces and led an uprising in Cuba against the colonizers; he was captured and burned at the stake in 1511. Tradition has it that when offered last rites by a Spanish priest so his soul could go to heaven, Hatuey asked if that's where the souls of the Spanish conquerors went. When he was assured it was, he declined the rites, saying he preferred his soul go elsewhere.

July 26 Revolutionary Movement – Founded June 1955 by Fidel Castro and other veterans of the Moncada and Bayamo attack, youth activists from the left wing of the Orthodox Party, and other independent revolutionary forces; it separated from the Orthodox Party in March 1956. During the revolutionary war it was composed of the Rebel Army in the mountains (*Sierra*) and the urban underground network (*Llano*), as well as revolutionists in exile. In May 1958 Fidel Castro became its general secretary. It published the newspaper *Revolución,* beginning in clandestinity.

In 1961 the July 26 Movement fused with the Popular Socialist Party and the Revolutionary Directorate to form the Integrated Revolutionary Organizations (ORI). In 1963 the ORI took the name United Party of the Socialist Revolution (PURS); in 1965 the Communist Party of Cuba was founded, with Fidel Castro as first secretary.

Kabila, Laurent Desire (b. 1939) – Leader of the Congolese youth movement under Patrice Lumumba. He opposed the 1960 U.S.-backed coup that brought down the anti-imperialist government of the newly independent country, headed by Patrice Lumumba. Kabila helped lead the 1964 rebellion against the pro-imperialist regime of Joseph Kasavubu and Moise Tshombe. From exile Kabila was one of the Congolese leaders of the forces whom the Cuban internationalists led by Che Guevara assisted in 1965. He founded the People's Revolutionary Party in 1967. Following the ouster of Mobutu in 1997, Kabila became the country's head of state.

Kasavubu, Joseph (1917–1969) – President of the Congo under Patrice Lumumba. He supported the coup that ousted Lumumba in late 1960. In July 1964 Kasavubu appointed Moise Tshombe as prime minister, but dismissed him in October 1965. Kasavubu remained president until November 1965, when he himself was ousted in a coup by Joseph Mobutu.

La Coubre – A French ship carrying Belgian arms purchased by Cuba's revolutionary government with funds largely donated by Cuban working people. The ship blew up in Havana harbor on March 4, 1960, killing eighty-one people.

Lenin, V.I. (1870–1924) – Central leader of the 1917 October Revolution in Russia. Founder of the Bolshevik Party. Chair of the Council of People's Commissars (Soviet government) 1917–24; member of the Executive Committee of the Communist International.

López, Antonio "Ñico" (1934–1956) – A participant in the July 26, 1953, attack on the "Carlos Manuel de Céspedes" army garrison in Bayamo that took place simultaneously with the Moncada attack. He escaped arrest and lived in exile in Guatemala, where he became friends with Ernesto Guevara in 1954 and helped win him to the July 26 Movement. In 1955–56 he served as a member of the July 26 Movement's National Directorate and was head of its youth brigades. He participated in the *Granma* expedition in December 1956 and was captured and murdered by the army shortly after the landing. The leadership school of the Communist Party of Cuba is named after him.

Lorente, Miguel (b. 1937) – A native of Manzanillo, he joined the Rebel Army in the Sierra Maestra and rose to the rank of lieutenant in Camilo Cienfuegos's column. He took part in internationalist missions in Ethiopia and in Angola, where he participated in the Cuito Cuanavale campaign in 1988. A brigadier general of the FAR, he retired from active service in 1999.

Lumumba, Patrice (1925–1961) – Leader of the independence struggle in the Congo and its prime minister after independence from Belgium in June 1960. In September 1960, after requesting United Nations troops to block attacks by Belgian-organized mercenaries, his government was overthrown in a U.S.-backed coup. UN troops supposedly protecting Lumumba took no action as he was captured, jailed, and then murdered by rightist forces in January 1961.

Maceo, Antonio (1845–1896) – Prominent military leader and strategist in Cuba's wars of independence from Spain in the nineteenth century. He was a leader of the 1895–96 westward march from Oriente that culminated in the invasion of Pinar del Río province. He became a symbol of revolutionary intransigence in 1878, at the conclusion of Cuba's first independence war, when he refused to put down his arms against the colonial regime, issuing what became known as the Baraguá Protest. Popularly known in Cuba as the Bronze Titan, he was killed in battle December 7, 1896.

Machado, José R. ("Machadito") (b. 1930) – Member of the July 26 Movement and medical doctor, he joined the Rebel Army during the revolutionary war and served under Raúl Castro, attaining

the rank of commander. He was minister of public health 1960–
68, and first secretary of the Havana provincial committee of the
Communist Party 1971–76. He has been a member of the Central
Committee of the Communist Party since 1965. A long-time mem-
ber of the Political Bureau, he has been on the Central Committee
Secretariat since 1976. He is a member of the Council of State.

McNamara, Robert (b. 1916) – Secretary of defense in the Kennedy
administration during the 1962 October "Missile" Crisis and in
the Johnson administration during the Vietnam War.

Mambí – A reference to fighters in Cuba's wars of independence
from Spain, many of them freed slaves or agricultural workers.
The term "mambí" originated in the 1840s during the fight for
independence from Spain in the nearby island of Hispaniola. After a black Spanish officer named Juan Ethninius Mamby joined
the independence fighters in Hispaniola, Spanish forces began
referring to the guerrillas by the derogatory term "mambies." Later
the related term "mambises" was applied to the freedom fighters
in Cuba, who adopted it as a badge of honor.

Martí, José (1853–1895) – A noted poet, writer, speaker, and journalist, he is Cuba's national hero. He founded the Cuban Revolutionary Party in 1892 to fight Spanish rule and oppose U.S. de-
signs on Cuba. He organized and planned the 1895 independence
war and was killed in battle at Dos Ríos in Oriente. His revolutionary anti-imperialist program is part of the internationalist traditions and political heritage of the Cuban revolution.

Martínez Tamayo, José María (1936–1967) – Known at various
times by the noms de guerre of Mbili, Papi, and Ricardo. Worked
as Guevara's liaison with revolutionary forces in Latin America
beginning in 1962. He served with Guevara in the Congo and
then Bolivia, where he was in charge of the advance preparations
for the guerrilla front. He was killed in battle in June 1967.

Marx, Karl (1818–1883) – Founder with Frederick Engels (1820–
1895) of the modern communist workers movement.

Menéndez, Jesús (1911–1948) – General secretary of the National
Federation of Sugar Workers and a member of the Popular Socialist Party; murdered at the Manzanillo train station in January

1948 by police captain Joaquín Casillas. At the time the government of Cuba was under the bourgeois-democratic regime of President Ramón Grau San Martín.

Mobutu Sese Seko (1930-1997) – Named chief of staff by Patrice Lumumba in the former Belgian colony of the Congo, Mobutu led a coup in September 1960. Following the murder of Lumumba in January 1961, Mobutu became the country's strongman. In 1965 he proclaimed himself president, holding power until he was overthrown in 1997. Born Joseph Mobutu, he changed his name to Mobutu Sese Seko in 1972.

Moncada garrison – On July 26, 1953, some 160 revolutionaries under the command of Fidel Castro launched an insurrectionary attack on the Moncada army garrison in Santiago de Cuba together with a simultaneous attack on the garrison in Bayamo, opening the revolutionary armed struggle against the Batista dictatorship. After the attack's failure, Batista's forces massacred more than fifty of the captured revolutionaries. Fidel Castro and twenty-seven others, including Raúl Castro and Juan Almeida, were tried and sentenced to up to fifteen years in prison. They were released on May 15, 1955, after a public defense campaign forced Batista's regime to issue an amnesty.

Montané, Jesús "Chucho" (1923–1999) – A leader of the 1953 Moncada attack, he was sentenced to ten years in prison and released in May 1955 following a national amnesty campaign. A participant in the *Granma* expedition, he was captured in December 1956 and held prisoner for the remainder of the war. Responsibilities he held from 1959 on included head of the Central Committee's International Department; organizer of the Central Committee; head of tourism; minister of communication. He was a member of Communist Party Central Committee from 1965 until his death.

Mulele, Pierre (1929–1968) – Education minister of the Congo in 1960 under Patrice Lumumba. Opposed the 1960 U.S.-backed coup that led to Lumumba's murder. He was secretary general of the African Solidarity Party and helped lead the 1964–65 rebellion against the pro-imperialist regime of Joseph Kasavubu and Moise Tshombe, heading the rebellion in Kwilu province, east of Leopoldville (today Kinshasa). Arrested by the regime of Mobutu Sese Seko after he accepted its offer of amnesty and returned to Kinshasa, he was shot by a firing squad.

Namibia – In 1920, by dint of a League of Nations mandate, Namibia (South-West Africa) came under South African control. In 1946 the United Nations called for South Africa to submit a new trusteeship agreement. This request was rejected by the government of South Africa, which maintained that the UN had no right to challenge its occupation of Namibia. In 1966 the UN General Assembly voted to strip South Africa of its mandate.

Namibia won its independence in 1990. A decisive factor contributing to this victory, together with the deepening mass struggle inside South Africa, was the defeat of the forces of the apartheid regime in Angola at the hands of the Angolan army, Cuban volunteers, and Namibian independence fighters.

Ochoa, Arnaldo (1940–1989) – From a peasant family, he joined the Rebel Army in early 1958. He participated in an internationalist mission in Venezuela in the 1960s and headed the Cuban military missions in Ethiopia in the late 1970s, Nicaragua 1983–86, and Angola 1987–88. He was a member of the Communist Party Central Committee 1965–89.

In June-July 1989 Ochoa, then a division general, and three other high-ranking officers of the Revolutionary Armed Forces and Ministry of the Interior were arrested, tried, convicted, and executed for hostile acts against a foreign state, drug trafficking, and abuse of office. He organized the smuggling of ivory and other goods while heading Cuba's military mission in Angola and had established contacts, through third parties, with international drug dealers. At the same trial, thirteen other Cuban army and Ministry of the Interior officers were convicted and given prison sentences.

October 1962 "Missile" Crisis – In the face of escalating preparations by Washington for an invasion of Cuba in the spring and summer of 1962, the Cuban government signed a mutual defense agreement with the Soviet Union. In October 1962 U.S. president John Kennedy demanded removal of Soviet nuclear missiles installed in Cuba following the signing of that pact. Washington ordered a naval blockade of Cuba, stepped up its preparations to invade, and placed U.S. armed forces on nuclear alert. Cuban workers and farmers mobilized in the millions to defend the revolution. Following an exchange of communications between Washington and Moscow, on October 28 Soviet premier Nikita Khrushchev, without consulting the Cuban government, announced his decision to remove the missiles.

Orthodox Party (Cuban People's Party) – Known as the *ortodoxos*, it was formed in 1947 as a radical-democratic bourgeois movement on a platform of opposition to U.S. imperialist domination of Cuba and government corruption. Its youth wing provided many of the initial cadres for the Moncada assault. Its official leadership moved rightward after Batista's 1952 coup, and the party fragmented.

País, Frank (1934–1957) – Vice president of the Federation of University Students in Oriente, he was the central leader of Oriente Revolutionary Action, later renamed Revolutionary National Action, which fused with the Moncada veterans and other forces to form the July 26 Movement in 1955. He was the central leader of July 26 Movement in Oriente province, national action coordinator of the July 26 Movement, and head of its urban militias. He was murdered by the dictatorship's forces July 30, 1957.

Pérez, Crescencio (1895–1986) – A member of a July 26 Movement cell in the Sierra Maestra prior to the *Granma* landing, he was one of the first peasants to join the Rebel Army, finishing the war as commander of Column 7. Following the triumph of the revolution he carried various responsibilities as a member of the Revolutionary Armed Forces.

Pérez Róspide, Luis (b. 1943) – As a teenager, in 1958 he joined a cell of the July 26 Movement at the U.S. naval base at Guantánamo Bay. Later that year he joined the Rebel Army, serving in the front led by Raúl Castro. After 1959 he remained in the FAR and participated in the fight against counterrevolutionary bands during the 1960s. In 1988 he became head of the Union of Military Industries, charged with production of military supplies. He holds the rank of brigadier general.

Playa Girón. See Bay of Pigs

Popular Socialist Party (PSP) – Name taken in 1944 by the Communist Party of Cuba founded in 1925. The PSP opposed the 1952 Batista coup and dictatorship but rejected the political course of the Moncada assault and of the July 26 Movement and Rebel Army in launching the revolutionary war in 1956–57. The PSP collaborated with the July 26 Movement in the final months of the struggle, with the goal of bringing down the Batista dictatorship. As the revolution deepened following the 1959 victory, the PSP, like the July 26 Movement and Revolutionary Directorate, went through political differentiation. In mid 1961 the Integrated Revolutionary Organizations (ORI) was formed by a fusion of the three groups, initiating a process that led in 1965 to the founding of the Communist Party of Cuba with Fidel Castro as first secretary.

Puebla, Delsa "Teté" (b. 1939) – A native of Yara, she was one of the first women to join the Rebel Army in July 1957, rising to the rank of lieutenant by the end of the revolutionary war. She remained in the FAR after 1959 and holds the rank of brigadier general.

Rebel Army – Organized by Fidel Castro to start the revolutionary war called for and prepared by the July 26 Movement. Began military operations against the Batista regime in December 1956 when the *Granma* landed in Oriente province. Its defeat of the Batista army forces in numerous decisive engagements, from July 1958 on especially, gave impetus to a revolutionary upsurge throughout Cuba and sealed the fate of the dictatorship. Rebel Army cadres became the backbone of the new revolutionary government that emerged in February 1959 and of the Revolutionary Armed Forces, formed in October 1959. They became the central leadership of Cuban working people in countryside and city as the anticapitalist and anti-imperialist struggle deepened.

Rectification – The rectification process in Cuba between 1986 and the early 1990s marked a turn away from increasing reliance on the economic management and planning policies used in the Soviet Union and Eastern Europe, which had become dominant in Cuba throughout the 1970s and early 1980s. At its height, rectification took on the character of a growing social movement led by

Cuba's most conscious and disciplined working people. It was a negation of the course and social forces that were to bring about the collapse of the Communist regimes and parties of Eastern Europe and the USSR. As the economic and political crisis that became known as the Special Period accelerated from 1990 on, many of the measures associated with the rectification process, such as the spread of volunteer work brigades to build badly needed housing, had to be shelved. But the working-class momentum of rectification made possible the survival of Cuba's revolutionary government through the most difficult years of the revolution in the early 1990s.

Revolutionary Armed Forces (FAR) – The continuator of the Rebel Army, which had been led by Fidel Castro to wage Cuba's revolutionary war in 1956-58. In October 1959 the FAR was established, consolidating under a single command structure the Rebel Army, as well as the Rebel Air Force, the Revolutionary Navy, and the Revolutionary National Police. Raúl Castro became head of the Ministry of the Revolutionary Armed Forces (MINFAR), a responsibility he has held ever since.

Revolutionary Directorate – Organization formed in 1955 by José Antonio Echeverría and other leaders of the Federation of University Students in the struggle against Batista. It organized an attack on Batista's Presidential Palace on March 13, 1957, in which a number of central leaders, including Echeverría, were killed. It organized a guerrilla column in the Escambray mountains in Las Villas in February 1958 led by Faure Chomón that fought under the command of Che Guevara in the last months of the revolutionary war. Through a process of splits and differentiations, it fused with the July 26 Movement and PSP in 1961 to form the Integrated Revolutionary Organizations that eventually led to the founding of the Communist Party of Cuba in 1965.

Rosales del Toro, Ulises (b. 1942) – Division general in the FAR. He joined the Rebel Army in 1957, serving under Juan Almeida. He carried out internationalist missions in Algeria and Venezuela 1963–68, and was assigned to Angola in 1976. He has been a member of Communist Party Central Committee since 1975, and is a member of the party's Political Bureau. Formerly the FAR's chief of staff and first substitute of the minister of the FAR, he was appointed sugar minister in October 1997.

Sánchez, Celia (1920–1980) – Born in Manzanillo, near the Sierra Maestra mountains of eastern Cuba, she was a founding member of the Orthodox Party in 1947 and a leader of its youth. She became a leader of the amnesty campaign in Oriente province for the Moncada prisoners. In 1955 she was a founding member of the July 26 Movement, and became its central organizer in Manzanillo. She organized the urban supply and recruitment network for the Rebel Army, and was the first woman to become a combatant in the Rebel Army, serving on its general command beginning October 1957. At her death she was a member of the Communist Party Central Committee and secretary of the Council of State and Council of Ministers.

Sorí Marín, Humberto – An Authentic Party politician, he joined the Rebel Army in the Sierra Maestra in 1957, ending the war with the rank of commander. After the revolution he was minister of agriculture from January to June 1959. Soon after the agrarian reform was enacted in May 1959, he left Cuba for the United States. He returned to join a counterrevolutionary band and was captured and executed in 1961.

Soto, Lionel (b. 1927) – Joined the Popular Socialist Party in 1946 at the University of Havana. He was imprisoned on the Isle of Pines during the revolutionary struggle. As part of the fusion process of the July 26 Movement, PSP and Revolutionary Directorate, he headed the Schools of Revolutionary Instruction 1960–67, and subsequently held various diplomatic and party posts. He was a member of the Communist Party Central Committee 1965–80 and 1991–97.

Soumialot, Gaston – A leader of the 1964–65 uprising in the Congo against the pro-imperialist regime. He was defense minister in the short-lived Congolese People's Republic proclaimed by the rebels.

Soviet-German pact – In August 1939 the governments of the Soviet Union and Germany concluded a nonaggression pact. As part of that agreement, on September 1, German imperialist troops

invaded Poland from the west, and Soviet troops occupied eastern Poland. The pact made it possible for Hitler's general staff to
march the Wehrmacht west without fear of a two-front war. Once
Western Europe had been conquered to the English Channel, Hitler
turned and invaded the Soviet Union in June 1941, catching the
Soviet government and Communist Party leadership by surprise.
Instead of using the time to strengthen defense of the Soviet Union
worldwide, Stalin and the Comintern leadership had deepened
illusions in Communist Parties everywhere in the supposedly
stable, long-term character of the "nonaggression" pact and had
brought the Moscow show trials to their bloody conclusion, finishing the purge of the Soviet officer corps that virtually decapi-
tated the Red Army.

In a 1992 interview with Nicaraguan revolutionary Tomás
Borge, Fidel Castro described these policies of Stalin prior to World
War II as "a flagrant violation of principles: to seek peace with
Hitler at any cost, stalling for time. . . . Far from gaining time, the
nonaggression pact shortened it, because war broke out anyway. . . .
If Hitler had declared war on the USSR in 1939, the destruction
would have been less than the destruction caused in 1941, and he
would have suffered the same fate as Napoleon Bonaparte. . . .
With the people's participation in an irregular war, the USSR would
have defeated Hitler." Stalin also "conducted a terrible bloody
purge of the armed forces, practically beheading the Soviet Army
on the eve of war," Castro noted.

Special Period – The term used in Cuba for the extremely difficult
economic conditions the Cuban people have faced since the early
1990s, and the policies the leadership has implemented in face of
them to defend the revolution. With the disintegration of the regimes of the Soviet-led Comecon (Council of Mutual Economic
Assistance) that previously accounted for 85 percent of Cuba's
foreign trade, much of it on terms favorable to Cuba, the island
was brutally thrust back into the world capitalist market from
which it had been partially sheltered for nearly 30 years. The sud-
den and unilateral break in trading patterns—which took place
as the world capitalist crisis intensified, and have been exacer-

bated by the heightened economic warfare organized by Washington—led to the most severe economic crisis in Cuba since 1959.

In 1993 and 1994 a number of measures were adopted to address the worsening economic conditions.

Steps included the opening of agricultural markets throughout the country in October 1994 so that individual family farmers, cooperatives, and state farms—after fulfilling delivery quotas to state distribution agencies at fixed prices—can sell surplus agricultural products directly to the population. Most Cubans purchase goods at these markets to supplement what is available, at lower prices, through rationing.

In September 1993 the government legalized self-employment in some 140 occupations, to provide services to the population unavailable from the state. Individuals receive licenses from the government and pay taxes on their income.

The UBPCs (Basic Units of Cooperative Production) were institutionalized in 1993, reorganizing the majority of state farms into smaller cooperative units, producing sugarcane, food crops, and other agricultural products.

In July 1993, the government made it legal for ordinary Cubans to hold and use U.S. dollars and other hard currency. Remittances from family members abroad were encouraged, and a network of stores opened where many essential products virtually unattainable for pesos could be purchased for dollars.

Joint ventures with foreign capital, especially in tourism and related production, expanded rapidly.

By 1996, through the efforts of Cuban working people, the decline in industrial and agricultural production bottomed out. Shortages of food and other essentials, though still severe, began to ease.

Tania (*Haydée Tamara Bunke*) (1937–1967) – Born in Argentina of a German father and Soviet-German mother who had fled Nazi Germany. In 1952 her family moved to the German Democratic Republic. She moved to Cuba 1961, working in the Ministry of Education and as a translator. In March 1963 she volunteered for internationalist duty and was trained in clandestine work. She was sent to Bolivia in November 1964, where she worked on advance preparations for the revolutionary front led by Che Guevara. In March 1967, while escorting visitors to the guerrilla camp, her cover was blown and she joined the unit as a combatant. She was killed August 31, 1967.

Verde Olivo (Olive drab) – Weekly magazine of Cuba's Revolutionary Armed Forces founded in 1959 under the guidance of the Department of Instruction headed by Che Guevara.

Yara, Grito de (Cry of Yara) – On October 10, 1868, Carlos Manuel de Céspedes, the owner of a sugar plantation at La Demajagua near the town of Manzanillo in southeastern Cuba, rang the sugar mill's bell, assembled the plantation slaves, and announced they were free. He invited them to join him in a fight to win Cuba's independence from Spain. Céspedes then formed up a contingent of fighters and attacked the Spanish forces in the nearby town of Yara. This act, known in Cuban history as *El Grito de Yara* (the Cry of Yara), was the beginning of Cuba's first war for independence, which lasted until 1878.

Further reading

Throughout the interviews with the generals in Making History, *the reader will encounter references to historical events and individuals that may be unfamiliar. Most of the following suggestions for further reading are available from Pathfinder.*

Almeida, Juan. Two trilogies have been published containing Almeida's memoirs of the Cuban revolutionary struggle. The first three books—entitled respectively *Presidio, Exilio,* and *Desembarco* [Prison, Exile, and The landing] (Havana: Editorial de Ciencias Sociales, 1987–88)—cover the period from the imprisonment of the Moncada combatants in 1953 through the *Granma* landing of December 1956. The second three—*La Sierra, Por las faldas del Turquino,* and *La Sierra Maestra y más allá* [The Sierra, Along the slopes of Mt. Turquino, and The Sierra Maestra and beyond] (Havana: Editora Política, 1989–95)—recount experiences during the 1956–58 revolutionary war.

Báez, Luis, *Secretos de generales* [Secrets of generals] (Havana: Fuerzas Armadas Revolucionarias, 1997). Interviews with forty-one generals of the Revolutionary Armed Forces—including López Cuba, Carreras, Fernández, and Villegas—in which they tell of their experiences during Cuba's revolutionary war, the 1961 battle at Playa Girón, internationalist missions, and other efforts to defend and strengthen the Cuban revolution.

Balaguer, José Ramón, "Socialism: A Viable Option" in *New International* no. 11 (1998). Opening presentation to the October 1997 international workshop on Socialism on the Threshold of the Twenty-first Century. Also available in *Cuba Socialista* no. 8.

Barnes, Jack and Clark, Steve, "The Politics of Economics: Che Guevara and Marxist Continuity" discusses the communist course pursued by Guevara from 1961 to 1965 as he led Cuban working people to begin transforming the economic foundations inherited from capitalism—and takes up debates among revolutionists since that time over the policies Guevara fought for. In *New International* no. 8 (1991), which also contains "Che's Proletarian Legacy and Cuba's Rectification Process" by Mary-Alice Waters, and two articles by Guevara written in 1963–64 as contributions to the debate over planning and management in Cuba.

Carreras, Enrique, *Por el dominio del aire: Memorias de un piloto de combate (1943–1988)* [Controlling the air: memoirs of a combat pilot 1943–1988] (Havana: Editora Política, 1995).

Cuba on the Brink: Castro, the Missile Crisis, and the Soviet Collapse edited by James Blight, Bruce Allyn, and David Welch (New York: Pantheon Books, 1993). Contains major portions of the transcripts of a conference on the October 1962 "Missile" Crisis held in Havana January 9–12, 1992, involving Fidel Castro and other contemporary participants in those events from the Cuban, U.S., and Soviet governments.

Castro, Fidel, speech at the ceremony in Santa Clara, October 17, 1997, when the remains of Guevara and fellow combatants killed in Bolivia were interred. In *Celebrating the Homecoming of Ernesto Che Guevara's Reinforcement Brigade to Cuba,* a collection of articles published in the *Militant* newsweekly (1997). The booklet also includes appreciations of Guevara by Ricardo Alarcón, Ahmed Ben Bella, and other revolutionists who knew and worked with him.

Castro, Fidel, "Cuba's Rectification Process: Two Speeches by Fidel Castro," in *New International* no. 6 (1986). Presents the aims of the rectification process and the necessity for it.

Castro, Fidel, *In Defense of Socialism: Four Speeches on the 30th Anniversary of the Cuban Revolution* (Pathfinder, 1989). Explains the political accomplishments of the rectification process and Cuba's internationalist aid to Angola. Defends Cuba's socialist course in contrast to what was fast unfolding in Eastern Europe and the USSR.

Castro, Fidel, *Cuba's Internationalist Foreign Policy 1975–80* (Pathfinder, 1981). Includes speeches on Cuba's aid to Angola and Ethiopia, support for the Nicaraguan revolution, efforts to strengthen the anti-imperialist forces within the Nonaligned Movement, and more.

Castro, Fidel, and Betto, Frei, *Fidel and Religion* (Simon and Schuster, 1987). This 1985 interview contains one of the fullest accounts of Castro's early life and how he became a revolutionary and a communist. It includes a description of his early years in Oriente province, his education in Jesuit-run schools, and the impact on him of the tradition of struggle in eastern Cuba.

Castro, Fidel and Guevara, Ernesto Che, *To Speak the Truth: Why Washington's 'Cold War' against Cuba Doesn't End* (Pathfinder, 1992). Using the platform of the United Nations, Castro and Guevara present the example of the Cuban revolution and speak to working people around the world who are fighting for national liberation and socialism. Among the topics addressed, both Cuban leaders speak of the esteem they had for Patrice Lumumba and his leadership of the anti-imperialist struggle in the Congo.

Castro, Raúl, *Selección de discursos y artículos, 1959–1986* [Selection of speeches and articles, 1959–1986], 2 vols. (Havana: Editora Política, 1988).

Castro, Raúl, and Guevara, Ernesto Che, *La conquista de la esperanza* [The conquest of hope] (Havana: Casa Editora Abril, 1996). First published in the 1980s, this book consists largely of excerpts from the diaries of these two young rebel leaders during the opening months of Cuba's revolutionary war.

Guevara, Ernesto Che, *Socialism and Man in Cuba* (Pathfinder, 1968, 1989). Guevara's 1965 essay discussing the fundamental political and economic questions facing the working class in transforming itself, as it leads the transition to socialism.

Guevara, Ernesto Che, *The Bolivian Diary of Ernesto Che Guevara* (Pathfinder, 1995). A day-by-day account, written as the struggle unfolded, of the effort led by Guevara to initiate a revolutionary front in the Southern Cone of Latin America in 1966–67.

Guevara, Ernesto Che, *Episodes of the Cuban Revolutionary War, 1956–58.* (Pathfinder, 1996). Guevara's account of the construction and education of the Rebel Army and the forging of a revolutionary leadership of the workers and peasants in Cuba. Also includes Guevara's 1965 letter to Fidel Castro, resigning his leadership positions and responsibilities in Cuba to join the revolutionary struggle in other parts of the world.

Guevara, Ernesto Che, *Pasajes de la guerra revolucionaria: Congo* [Episodes of the Congo revolutionary war] (Milan, Barcelona: Grijalbo-Mondadori, 1999). Guevara's previously unpublished first-hand account of the 1965 campaign by a Cuban volunteer detachment aiding anti-imperialist fighters in the Congo.

Mandela, Nelson and Castro, Fidel, *How Far We Slaves Have Come! Cuba and South Africa in Today's World* (Pathfinder, 1991). Speeches in Cuba, July 26, 1991, including Mandela's assessment of the significance of the 1988 battle of Cuito Cuanavale in southern Angola and Cuba's historic role in assisting the African freedom struggle.

Marx, Karl, and Engels, Frederick, "Revolutionary Spain," in Karl Marx and Frederick Engels, *Collected Works*, vol. 13 (Moscow: Progress Publishers, 1979), esp. pp. 400–439. In a series of articles written for the *New York Daily Tribune*, Marx draws lessons from the popular war of resistance within Spain to the rule of Joseph Bonaparte, brother of Napoleon, who was proclaimed king of Spain in 1808 and driven out in 1813.

Villegas, Harry, *Pombo: A Man of Che's 'guerrilla'* (Pathfinder, 1997). Villegas's diary and account of the 1966–68 revolutionary campaign in Bolivia.

Vindicación de Cuba (Havana: Editora Política, 1989) and *Case 1/1989: End of the Cuban Connection* (Havana: José Martí Foreign Language Publishing House, 1989). Provide a documentary record of the 1989 trial of Arnaldo Ochoa and thirteen other high-ranking officers in the Revolutionary Armed Forces and Ministry of the Interior.

Waters, Mary-Alice, "Defending Cuba, Defending Cuba's Socialist Revolution" in *New International* no. 10 (1994). Defends the communist course of the Cuban leadership in meeting the challenges posed by the Special Period.

Index

The Cuban revolution

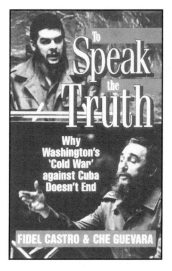

To Speak the Truth
Why Washington's 'Cold War' against Cuba Doesn't End
Fidel Castro and Che Guevara
In historic speeches before the United Nations and UN bodies, Guevara and Castro address the workers of the world, explaining why the U.S. government so hates the example set by the socialist revolution in Cuba and why Washington's efforts to destroy it will fail. $16.95

Dynamics of the Cuban Revolution
A Marxist Appreciation
Joseph Hansen
How did the Cuban revolution come about? Why does it represent, as Hansen puts it, an "unbearable challenge" to U.S. imperialism? What political challenges has it confronted? Written as the revolution advanced from its earliest days. $20.95

How Far We Slaves Have Come!
South Africa and Cuba in Today's World
Nelson Mandela and Fidel Castro
Speaking together in Cuba in 1991, Mandela and Castro discuss the unique relationship and revolutionary example of the struggles of the South African and Cuban peoples. Also available in Spanish. $9.95

Celebrating the Homecoming of Ernesto Che Guevara's Reinforcement Brigade to Cuba
Articles from the *Militant* newspaper on the 30th anniversary of the combat waged in Bolivia by Che and his comrades. Available in English and Spanish. $8.00

in today's world

Che Guevara, Cuba, and the Road to Socialism

Articles by Ernesto Che Guevara, Carlos Rafael Rodríguez, Carlos Tablada, Mary-Alice Waters, Steve Clark, Jack Barnes

Exchanges from the early 1960s and today on the political perspectives defended by Guevara as he helped lead working people to advance the transformation of economic and social relations in Cuba. In *New International* no. 8. $10.00

Che Guevara and the Imperialist Reality

Mary-Alice Waters

"The world of capitalist disorder—the imperialist reality of the 21st century—would not be strange to Che," Waters explains. "Far from being dismayed by the odds we face, he would have examined the world with scientific precision and charted a course to win." In English and Spanish. Pamphlet. $3.00

Episodes of the Cuban Revolutionary War, 1956–58

Ernesto Che Guevara

A firsthand account of the military campaigns and political events that culminated in the January 1959 popular insurrection that overthrew the Batista dictatorship. With clarity and humor, Guevara describes his own political education. He explains how the struggle transformed the men and women of the Rebel Army and July 26 Movement led by Fidel Castro. And how these combatants forged a political leadership capable of guiding millions of workers and peasants to open the socialist revolution in the Americas. $23.95

Secretos de generales
(Secrets of Generals)
A collection of interviews by Luis Báez with 41 top officers of Cuba's armed forces. They tell how they joined the revolutionary movement to overthrow the U.S.-backed Batista dictatorship in the 1950s and discuss their experiences around the world fighting alongside national liberation movements in Africa, Asia, and Latin America. In Spanish, $29.95

In Defense of Socialism
Fidel Castro

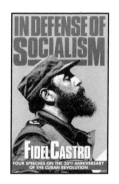

Four Speeches on the 30th Anniversary of the Cuban Revolution, 1988–89
Economic and social progress is possible without the dog-eat-dog competition of capitalism, Castro argues, and socialism remains the only way forward for humanity. Also discusses Cuba's role in the struggle against the apartheid regime in southern Africa. $13.95

Pombo: A Man of Che's *guerrilla*
With Che Guevara in Bolivia, 1966–68
Harry Villegas
A never-before-published story of the 1966–68 revolutionary campaign in Bolivia led by Ernesto Che Guevara. This is the diary and account of a young fighter, still in his twenties, who was a member of Guevara's general staff. Villegas's account of this epic chapter in the history of the America's foreshadows the titanic class battles that will mark the 21st century. $21.95

Pasajes de la guerra revolucionaria: Congo
(Episodes of the Congo Revolutionary War)
Ernesto Che Guevara
Published for the first time in 1999, Guevara's account presents the central lessons of the Cuban volunteer contingent that fought alongside anti-imperialist forces in the Congo in 1965 and discusses the prospects for revolutionary struggle in Africa. In Spanish, $23.95

Revolution in Central America and the Caribbean

The Rise and Fall of the Nicaraguan Revolution

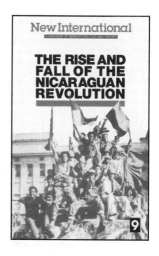

Socialist Workers Party resolutions and articles by Jack Barnes, Steve Clark, and Larry Seigle

Lessons from the victory and defeat of the workers and peasants government that came to power in July 1979. Based on ten years of working-class journalism from inside Nicaragua, this special issue of *New International* magazine recounts the achievements and worldwide impact of the Nicaraguan revolution. It traces the political retreat of the Sandinista leadership that led to the revolution's downfall at the end of the 1980s. Includes the "Historic Program of the FSLN." $14.00

The Second Assassination of Maurice Bishop

by Steve Clark

The lead article in *New International* no. 6 reviews the accomplishments of the 1979–83 revolution in the Caribbean island of Grenada. Explains the roots of the 1983 coup that led to the murder of revolutionary leader Maurice Bishop, and to the destruction of the workers and farmers government by a Stalinist political faction within the governing New Jewel Movement.

Also in *New International* no. 6: Washington's Domestic Contra Operation *by Larry Seigle* • Renewal or Death: Cuba's Rectification Process *two speeches by Fidel Castro* • Land, Labor, and the Canadian Revolution *by Michel Dugré* $15.00

Distributed by Pathfinder

Also from Pathfinder

Jack Barnes
CAPITALISM'S WORLD DISORDER
WORKING-CLASS POLITICS AT THE MILLENNIUM

Capitalism's World Disorder

Working-Class Politics at the Millennium

JACK BARNES

The social devastation, financial panic, political turmoil, police brutality, and acts of imperialist aggression accelerating around us are not chaos. They are the product of lawful—and understandable—forces unleashed by capitalism. But the future the propertied classes have in store for us is not inevitable. It can be changed by the timely solidarity, courageous action, and united struggle of workers and farmers conscious of their power to tranform the world. $23.95

The Changing Face of U.S. Politics

Working-Class Politics and the Trade Unions

JACK BARNES

A handbook for workers coming into the factories, mines, and mills, as they react to the uncertain life, ceaseless turmoil, and brutality of capitalism today. It shows how millions of workers, as political resistance grows, will revolutionize themselves, their unions, and their conditions of life and work. Also available in Spanish and French. $19.95

JACK BARNES
THE CHANGING FACE OF U.S. POLITICS
Working-class politics and the unions

The Communist Manifesto

KARL MARX AND FREDERICK ENGELS

Founding document of the modern working-class movement, published in 1848. Explains why communism is derived not from preconceived principles but from facts and from proletarian movements springing from the actual class struggle. $3.95

KARL MARX
FREDERICK ENGELS
The
COMMUNIST
MANIFESTO

Write for a catalog. See front of book for addresses.

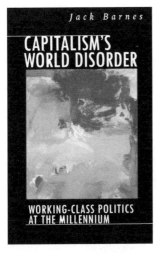

The History of the Russian Revolution

LEON TROTSKY

The social, economic, and political dynamics of the first socialist revolution as told by one of its central leaders. Unabridged, 3 vols. in one. $35.95

Malcolm X Talks to Young People

"I for one will join in with anyone, I don't care what color you are, as long as you want to change this miserable condition that exists on this earth"—Malcolm X, Britain, December 1964. Also includes his 1965 interview with the *Young Socialist* magazine. $10.95

Socialism on Trial

JAMES P. CANNON

The basic ideas of socialism, explained in testimony during the trial of 18 leaders of the Minneapolis Teamsters union and the Socialist Workers Party framed up and imprisoned under the notorious Smith "Gag" Act during World War II. $15.95

Puerto Rico: Independence Is a Necessity

RAFAEL CANCEL MIRANDA

"Our people are becoming aware of their own strength, which is what the colonial powers fear," explains Puerto Rican independence leader Rafael Cancel Miranda. In two interviews, Cancel Miranda—one of five Puerto Rican Nationalists imprisoned by Washington for more than 25 years until 1979—speaks out on the brutal reality of U.S. colonial domination, the campaign to free Puerto Rican political prisoners, the example of Cuba's socialist revolution, and the resurgence of the independence movement today. In English and Spanish. $3.00

Teamster Rebellion

FARRELL DOBBS

The 1934 strikes that built the industrial union movement in Minneapolis and helped pave the way for the CIO, recounted by a central leader of that battle. The first in a four-volume series on the class-struggle leadership of the strikes and organizing drives that transformed the Teamsters union in much of the Midwest into a fighting social movement and pointed the road toward independent labor political action. $16.95

Socialism: Utopian and Scientific

FREDERICK ENGELS

Modern socialism is not a doctrine, Engels explains, but a working-class movement growing out of the establishment of large-scale capitalist industry and its social consequences. $4.00

Thomas Sankara Speaks

The Burkina Faso Revolution, 1983–87
Peasants and workers in the West African country of Burkina Faso established a popular revolutionary government and began to combat the hunger, illiteracy, and economic backwardness imposed by imperialist domination. Thomas Sankara, who led that struggle, explains the example set for all of Africa. $18.95

Black Music, White Business

Illuminating the History and Political Economy of Jazz

FRANK KOFSKY

Probes the economic and social conflicts between the artistry of Black musicians and the control by largely white-owned business of jazz distribution—the recording companies, booking agencies, festivals, clubs, and magazines. $15.95

From Pathfinder

Lenin's Final Fight

Speeches and Writings, 1922–23

V.I. LENIN

In the early 1920s Lenin waged a
political battle in the leadership of the
Communist Party of the USSR to
maintain the course that had enabled the
workers and peasants to overthrow the
tsarist empire, carry out the first successful socialist revolution, and begin
building a world communist movement.
The issues posed in Lenin's political fight
remain at the heart of world politics
today. Also available in Spanish.
$19.95

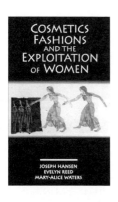

Cosmetics, Fashions, and the Exploitation of Women

JOSEPH HANSEN, EVELYN REED, AND
MARY-ALICE WATERS

How big business promotes cosmetics to
generate profits and perpetuate the oppression of
women. In her introduction, Waters explains how
the entry of millions of women into the workforce
during and after World War II irreversibly
changed U.S. society and laid the basis for a
renewed rise of struggles for women's equality.
$12.95

Out Now!

A Participant's Account of the Movement in the
United States against the Vietnam War

FRED HALSTEAD

The story of the political fight for a course that
could organize in action the maximum number of
working people, GIs, and youth and help lead the
growing international opposition to the Vietnam
War. Gaining momentum from the fight for Black
civil rights, the antiwar movement helped force the
U.S. government to bring the troops home,
spurring struggles for social justice and changing the political face of the
United States. $30.95

Write for a catalog. See addresses in front of book.

U.S. Imperialism Has Lost the Cold War . . .

New International

A MAGAZINE OF MARXIST POLITICS AND THEORY

U.S. IMPERIALISM HAS LOST THE COLD WAR

Jack Barnes

SOCIALISM: A VIABLE OPTION
by Jose Ramon Balaguer
YOUNG SOCIALISTS MANIFESTO

11

. . . That's what the Socialist Workers Party concluded a decade ago, in the wake of the collapse of regimes and parties across Eastern Europe and in the USSR that claimed to be Communist. Contrary to imperialism's hopes, the working class in those countries had not been crushed. It remains an intractable obstacle to reimposing and stabilizing capitalist relations, one that will have to be confronted by the exploiters in class battles—in a hot war.

Three issues of the Marxist magazine *New International* analyze the propertied rulers' failed expectations and chart a course for revolutionaries in response to the renewed rise of worker and farmer resistance to the economic and social instability, spreading wars, and rightist currents bred by the world market system. They explain why the historic odds in favor of the working class have increased, not diminished, at the opening of the 21st century.

New International no. 11

U.S. Imperialism Has Lost the Cold War *by Jack Barnes* • Socialism: A Viable Option *by José Ramón Balaguer* • Young Socialists Manifesto $14.00

New International no. 10

Imperialism's March toward Fascism and War *by Jack Barnes* • What the 1987 Stock Market Crash Foretold • Defending Cuba, Defending Cuba's Socialist Revolution *by Mary-Alice Waters* • The Curve of Capitalist Development *by Leon Trotsky* $14.00

New International no. 7

Opening Guns of World War III: Washington's Assault on Iraq *by Jack Barnes* • 1945: When U.S. Troops Said "No!" *by Mary-Alice Waters* • Lessons from the Iran-Iraq War *by Samad Sharif* $12.00

Distributed by Pathfinder

Many articles in **New International** are also available in Spanish in **Nueva Internacional**, in French in **Nouvelle Internationale**, and in Swedish in **Ny International**.